kids in the kitchen

charles lytton

Printed in the United States of America
First Edition

Charles Lytton
mulberrymoonshine@yahoo.com

Book design by PenworthyLLC

ISBN: 978-0-692-36172-6

Cooking with kids is
not just about ingredients,
recipes, and cooking.
It's about harnessing
imagination, empowerment,
and creativity.

Guy Fieri

So, true!

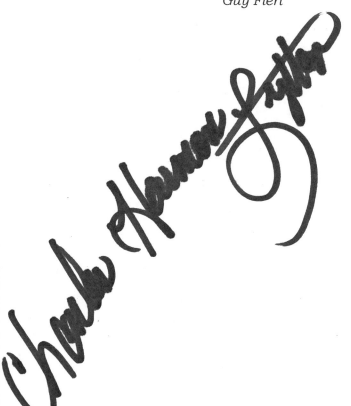

So true!

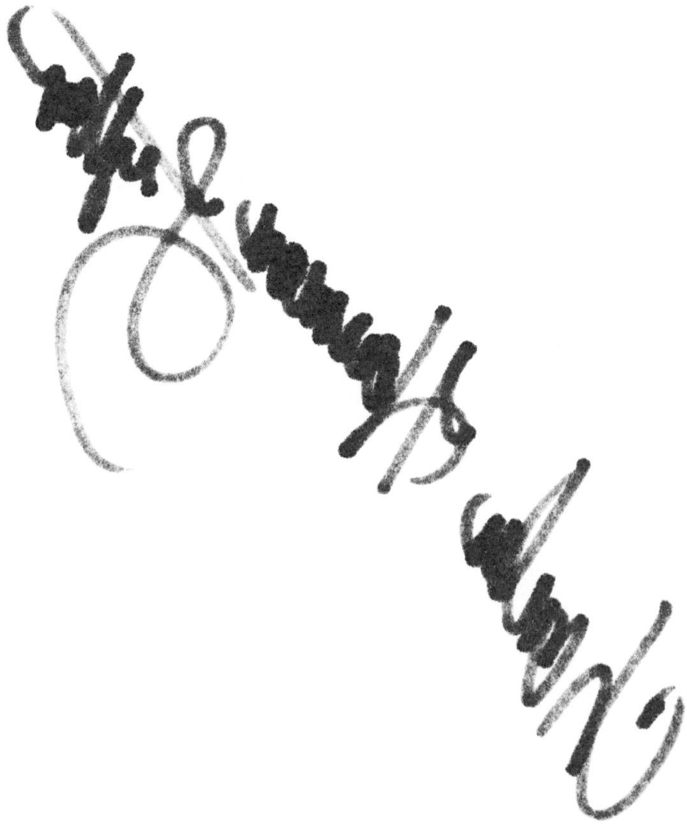

CONTENTS

Dedication

There are six little girls I truly enjoy watching cook! Five are my little granddaughters, and the other my only niece. Miss Rebecca, my little niece, is an amateur chef! She teaches me something every time I see her. She is fast and does things simply.

Tyler, Lilly and Charlie truly know what is going on. They measure carefully like they are measuring gold, and sometimes will stick their tongues out to help hold their hands still.

Avery and Brooke are still more in the "I can do this" phase, but they are catching on fast. They are true Christmas cookie magicians.

All are as pretty as their grandmother.

TO BEGIN WITH

Introduction

I have never thought of myself as a cook or a writer, for that matter. It's true that I have cooked for myself all of my life, and I have watched both my mother and my grandmother cook. When I was living in my little cinderblock cabin down on the banks of New River, I pretty much lived out of the garden, fish from the river and deer meat from the surrounding forest. I learned to like wild duck, too. Since I was always short on money and long on hunger, I found something to eat, I fixed it and ate it. When I had "dinner guests," some came back for seconds, while others found a new path up over the hill and are still running!

One day, a large group of people just descended on me. By chance, I had a two-gallon pot of pinto beans on the stove. My plan was to eat them all the coming week, but instead I saw bowl after bowl go out the front door. Everything was eaten: beans, chow-chow, and cornbread—everything.

Since I had to start over, I decided to do something a little different. I dumped as much black pepper in the bean pot as I could take. It may have been two tablespoons. Now, that slowed down the pinto-bean eating. It almost stopped me, too, but after a while I found I liked the black pepper. To this day I eat black pepper on about everything I fix.

When, despite the pepper, people kept coming and kept eating, I started cooking food that no one but me would eat. I cooked Mountain Oysters, lots of greens and boiled fish soup.

(If you don't know about Mountain Oysters, you can get the gist by reading my book, *New River: bonnets, apple butter and moonshine.*

I also learned that sometimes it is not about taste, but about looks. Once when old "Hammer Head," who'd been a friend for a good long time, came over early one morning to help raise trot lines, I made him breakfast. I cracked two eggs in a pan full of boiling water. Poor old Hammer Head went running outside to catch some air before his cookies came up. After he quit retching, he said them was the worst-looking eggs he had ever seen. He asked me how I got them watery-looking horns to stand on the eggs. I had eaten them and had not died, but Hammer Head wasn't taking any chances. I ate his, too.

During that phase of my life I was no longer a "fat little boy," but more on the order of a right manly type of man. I did not miss many meals, and I have eaten up some real funny concoctions and enjoyed almost every one of them. Just ask around.

When they get curious about just how I came up with some of my dishes, would-be gourmands sooner or later ask, "Did your grandmother and mother cook with a lot of herbs and spices?" The truth is, I think Mother was ahead of her time with spicing food. Grandmother used spices, too, but they were more of the readily available kind, what I generally call "pickling spices": garlic and salt and pepper. Mother grew up in Richmond, Virginia, and she had traveled around the East Coast before she and my father met. She was exposed to more foods and spices. For example, she always wanted me to plant "salsifer" [salsify] in the garden. I never could get it to take holt. Once or twice Chuck Shorter did get some salsifer going. He liked to pronounce salsifer with the Richmond accent like my mother always used. Mother liked to use spices, but poor

Elmer did not like much of anything but salt and very little black pepper, so she had to sneak around with spices and herbs.

The recipes listed in *Kids in the Kitchen* are some that both Mother and Grandmother prepared as well as others that I now have become accustomed to fixing and eating. A few are foods I have eaten in other homes and restaurants. Some are foods I hope to never eat again, but they are fun to talk about, now that my irritable bowel syndrome has cleared up a mite.

Important Questions I Am Always Being Asked

True Appalachians usually get how I cook, but some who've only been in these parts 30 or so years or somehow have not been paying attention ask questions that make me feel like I might need to clear up some issues before we begin.

Why do you always use a cast iron pan? I grew up watching Grandmother, Mother, Aunt Maude, and Aunt Tootie cook in cast iron pans. They all used cast iron because that is what they had. By the time I was ten or eleven, Mother had gotten a set of aluminum pans. Those are still in use today. But for me, I guess it is the old habits that are hardest to break. I am now old, and it is very hard to teach an old fat man new tricks, very hard indeed. Once there were a few people who had some success teaching "old dogs' new tricks." A few have tried the teaching thing on me. It just did not take much. It was like my old hands wouldn't answer.

In fact, I still use the same old cast iron egg skillet that my mother did. Some of my other cast iron skillets were saved from the dog lots on River Ridge. When a man on TV started advertising new types of skillets, many of the folks on the Ridge pitched their old-timey cast iron skillets out and took to using them as dog pans. Me, I went to the dog lots, top shelves of the cellars and farm shops and picked up the old cast iron pots and pans, and I've kept them.

How do you keep eggs from sticking in a cast iron skillet?

I do not want to turn this answer into a middle-school science project, so all I am going to say is that in a cast iron pan the iron molecules are big ones and there are small gaps between molecules. So you add lard, olive oil or vegetable shortening to the skillet and let it melt. As the pan heats up, the carbon in the oils fill in the voids between the iron molecules. If you do not let the pan heat up, the carbon atoms in the egg whites will fill these voids. This is sticking. And, of course, cast iron pans are seasoned to help reduce the sticking or temporarily fill these spaces. I can cook an egg as smoothly in cast iron as in one of those newer kinds of non-stick pans. In my cast iron skillet, you have to chase the fried egg to get it out of the pan and onto the plate. Me, I have one cast iron pan that is for cooking nothing but eggs!

How do you season a new cast iron frying pan?

This will take a few lines but seasoning can be done in 30 minutes. I think that there is a trend back to using cast iron cookware and away from some of those new fancy types of cookware. I am often told by people attending book signings that they have a cast iron pan and they used it a few times but they never could get the pan seasoned. “Why is that Mr. Lytton?” they ask.

See the section shown above. Here is my response. It takes a few minutes to season a cast iron skillet. If it is done correctly, foods will not stick. So here is what you do.

Set your cast iron pan in a sink of soapy water and wash it well. If it is a new pan, it might have oils on it from the manufacturer and lots of dust if it has been in the kitchen cabinet, but still wash it clean.

Next I rinse the cast iron pan with clean cold water to get rid of all the soap. Inspect the pan, and if it still is dirty, wash it again. Dry the clean pan and set it out on the counter to cool off and air dry.

I like to put a piece of aluminum foil across the bottom rack in the oven. This is to catch anything that might drip off the pan when it is seasoning.

I now paint the inside and outside of the pan with regular corn oil, before I turn it upside down in the oven. Make sure the skillet is centered over the aluminum foil. Turn the oven on to 325^0 and let the pan cook for about 45 minutes.

After the pan has cooked, I leave it in the oven to cool down, before taking it out of the oven and wiping it out with a paper towel. When it's dry, I pour one or two tablespoons of cooking oil into the pan and rub it all over the cooking surface. You can use lard, corn oil or olive oil. I think of this step as maintenance of the cast iron pan.

When it comes time to clean the pan after cooking something, I wipe it out with a paper towel and add a thin layer of vegetable oil for storage. I do not put the pan in soapy water. Soap destroys the seasoning. Every once in while you just need to re-season your cast iron pans.

Did your family honestly bury vegetables for winter? Can this be done today?

On River Ridge, about everyone had a big mound in the garden close to the house. In the early fall when that garden was cleaned out, vegetables had to be stored or canned. Once the potato bins were filled in the cellar, all the rest went to the earthen mound. Spring was fried and made into coleslaw. Fall cabbage was made into sauerkraut until all the jars were full.

Whatever was left went to the burial mound. Carrots, beets and onions were buried, too.

We did this by digging a shallow hole and lining it with fresh straw and hay. First, we put clean dry potatoes, onions and cabbage on the straw. Then, we added a second layer of vegetables and a second layer of straw. We covered the straw and vegetables with about 12 inches of soil shaped a lot like a cone so the water would drain off. Vegetables would stay fresh almost all of the winter.

I have read that some people today are doing this again. Today, I do not bury vegetables the way I once did, but now I bury dahlia bulbs for winter storage.

How do you make sausage?

People who have read my four earlier books sometimes call me and e-mail me with this kind of question. Such questions can take up 20 or 30 minutes at a book-signing. One lady wrote in a letter: "We have raised a hog in the back lot and want to cure hams and make sausage. My question is simple, 'Just how do you go about making sausage anyway?'"

I like to write and sell books, and don't want to upset my readers, really I don't, so my pat answer to this question is: *If you are not accustomed to killing hogs and working up meat, you need to talk with your local butcher or an old neighbor for an answer.* But, here is how I still do it, beginning to end.

All right, think about this. Hog killing is a day or two off. Get the neighbors and clean out the meat house and pay special attention to the bench where the meat is to be cut up and the place for the hams, middlings and shoulders.

Once the hog has been killed and dunked into the scalding

barrel and had all of the hair pulled off, it is time for it to be blocked out or cut into the hams, middlings (that's the side of the hog with the ribs attached) and shoulders. We identify what part of a bench is the sausage-making location. As we trim off the extra red meat or fat from the hams, shoulder and middlings, we pitch it into a trimming pile in the "sausage making location." Later, we will cut the skin off each piece of meat to make cracklings and lard.

When we are finished, we look the "sausage meat" over. When we are ready to start, we pull out the old family recipe for sausage seasoning and dust about 1/3 of the agreed-upon amount over the meat. With our hands, we stir the meat up and cover it again with about 1/3 of the family recipe. Then we do this another time.

We grind up the equivalence of three or four sausage cakes and cook them. It is best to eat them with hot biscuits and maybe even a pan of gravy. Now the family confirms the spices are right. If not, we go back to adding more red pepper or more sage or whatever. In Long Shop or on River Ridge (which is in Southwest Virginia, where I grew up), it is real hard to get too much sage in sausage.

Once we decide we've got it right, the grinding starts, and after that comes the canning or making links or freezing.

Again, ask for help from someone with experience. Today, people with no experience just want to watch how it is all done. Some people say it was Mark Twain who insisted you should never watch sausage or laws being made. Others insist it was that German fella, Otto von Bismarck. Whoever said it probably was right.

But what about the hams? Once we've trimmed all the sausage meat off the ham and other pieces, we set the ham on down on the table and rub it with a salt and sugar combination. In three weeks we have salt-cured ham, something I still like even though my blood pressure may not. I also like the salt, red pepper and sugar cure during which the ham is wrapped up in a white cotton sack for a year. *GO see someone with experience!*

How do you fix possum?

My answer is simple and quick. "I don't, and I ain't going to!"

For those people who just won't give up and say: "Well, please give me a few suggestions on how to eat a possum," I'm downright honest. To my knowledge I have eaten opossum only two times in my life. Mind you, I did not know a possum was an opossum until I was way up in high school. On River Ridge they are still just possums.

First off, you have got to catch a possum. Be real careful: they have a lot of teeth. Then you might do what the old timers did—put a fresh-caught possum in a rabbit cage for a few weeks and feed it clean table scraps, lots of clean green grass and all the clean water it can drink. A little corn is good, too. Old timers say: "A possum is a very dirty eater. The rascal will eat about anything, including your fingers if you get too close. So you need to cage that varmint for a while to clean him out."

After this you are on your own!

My only other suggestion is to find opossum in a cookbook that talks about nothing but cooking wild game, and then follow the recipe to the letter!

Finally, please don't ask me over for supper for a while. I just don't want to eat much more of it. I can still see them in my sleep after writing this. Still, if you insist, look on down a few pages; I have included two opossum recipes.

Where do you get your moonshine?

Well, I purchase my moonshine from the State ABC Store. "Why?" you might ask. I know it is clean, and it is relatively cheap compared to the cost of making licker. Most importantly, I don't use too much these days.

At book signings, group meetings and any gathering of people I am asked about moonshine. I do think that it is part of our culture. But be real careful with moonshine. You must know who has made it. A lot of knowledge and skills are required. If you ain't careful, you could come home with some of that "Old Head Bust"!

I still suggest you go over to the ABC Store.

Mr. Lytton, what in the world do you mean when you say, "fixed or cooked in the River Ridge or Long Shop Style?"

I think that living on River Ridge I observed a unique cooking style. My grandmother had ten children, so when she was cooking meals she didn't spend much time on how pretty the meal was or such niceties as the balance between the item to be cooked, herbs and seasonings. Meals had to be easy, nutritious and tasty. Inexpensive, too. What I am wishing to convey is simple food like my family prepared and ate living on River Ridge. We ate what we harvested—and ate all we could eat.

GOOD MORNING
SUNSHINE!

Brooke's and Sweet Baby Ray's Scrambled Eggs

One of the best foods in all the world are scrambled eggs! Miss Tyler, Lillian, Charlie and Avery all have mastered the fine art of this dish. But possibly the best scrambled eggs ever come from the kitchen of Brooke, or as all of her cousins call her, "Brookie." Brookie is three years old and already shows an interest in cooking. She has her own little apron and chef's hat, too. Judging by her eggs, she going to be a pretty good cook, too.

Here is what you need:

Have all of this stuff laid out on the counter before you start. Including your mother.

1 very, very patient mother or grandmother!

1 oven mitten

1 egg flipper

1 egg whisk or spatula

1 six-inch cast iron skillet

2 eggs

3 Tablespoons whole milk

2 Tablespoons olive oil

1 mixing bowl

3 cubes (¼-inch) American cheese

Some, but not much, dill weed, black pepper, garlic powder (Most likely no more than 1/8 teaspoon of any of these will be needed, but you be the judge of that.)

Salt? That is up to you.

Here is what you do:

1. Set the skillet on the stove eye on medium heat. Add the olive oil to the skillet. I like to use the back eyes of the stove or range. It is just me, but I think it is a little safer for a small child.

2. Crack the two eggs into the mixing bowl. (Save the eggshells to feed the worms in the compost.

3. Add the milk to the bowl.

4. Add the dill weed, black pepper, garlic powder. Salt now, if you want to.

5. Whisk up the eggs and milk until they are evenly mixed, and let them set for few minutes while the frying pan warms up. You may want to set the mixing bowl back in the refrigerator while the skillet warms up.

6. When the olive oil is bubbling, slowly pour the egg mixture into the pan. Never know, but this just might be a job for Mom.

7. Stir the eggs slowly for about one minute.
8. Add in the cheese cubes.
9. Here is one of my egg-cooking secrets. I take the skillet off the eye and put it on one of the other NON-HEATED stove eyes. The residual heat in the cast iron skillet is enough to finish cooking the eggs.
10. I like to cook my eggs until they are cooked all the way through, but not burned.

Notes for the cook's eyes only:

- There isn't anything better than a tall glass of sweet milk with scrambled eggs.
- Once in a while, I will add a slice of yellow American cheese to eggs. That is always a crowd-pleaser.

Pancakes Long Shop Style

When I was young, Mother made pancakes for breakfast. She did this three or four times a week. I could kind of tell where the weekly or monthly finances were by the number of times I ate pancakes. I just loved them and could have eaten them every morning, but when we started eating them for lunch and supper I knew Momma was tightening up the old money belt. Me, I just kept my mouth shut except when I opened it up to put in more butter-soaked pancakes. A meal like this one will get you all the way to lunch without any trouble.

Here is what you need:

One large cast iron skillet

3 cups all-purpose flour

2 Tablespoons white sugar

4 Tablespoons baking powder

1 Tablespoon salt

2 fresh eggs — (brown eggs, I hope)

1 or maybe 2 cups fresh whole milk. (You may need the second cup later, so hold off on using it right off.)

½ cup cream skimmed off the earthen crock in the

refrigerator

Some lard for the cast iron skillet

Butter and syrup for the stack of pancakes

A hard sour apple grated on the cabbage grater

Today, if is late in the day I will mix in 2 Tablespoons bourbon

Here is what you do:

1. Put a spoonful of lard in the cast iron skillet to warm up and melt.
2. Grate up your big apple and hold onto it.
3. In a large mixing bowl, sift the flour, sugar, baking powder and salt and set it out of the way.
4. In a second bowl, mix together eggs, cream and milk. (Bourbon too.) Add the apples to the batter now.
5. Dump the liquid and apples into the large flour bowl and mix a few times. DON'T over mix (If the batter needs a little more milk, now is the time to pour it in)
6. Slowly spoon the pancake batter into the hot cast iron skillet. When the pancakes start to bubble, carefully turn them over and cook until they are as brown as a chestnut.
7. If the cooking pan gets dry and the pancakes take to wanting to stick, just add in a little more lard.

Notes for the cook's eyes only;

- Stack up about six or seven on a plate.

- Place a hunk of yellow cow butter between each pancake. You may need to run a long broom straw down through the top to hold them up while the butter is melting.
- I like to fry Sunnyside Up two home-grown brown eggs, and I put them right on the top of the stack of pancakes.
- I cover the eggs and pancakes with Karo syrup.
- I always like a tall glass of sweet milk and four or five sausage cakes, too.
- That strong Luzianne coffee is good as well.

Fried Eggs

the Way They Are Eaten All Over Long Shop

There is no way to tell you just how many eggs I have eaten. When I was big enough to carry a small zinc bucket and fight off a mad hen gathering the eggs became my job. My egg-gathering started at grandmother's. She had a large chicken house with no less that fifty maybe seventy five pullets, roosters, layers and old hens. Some times of the year there could have been more sometimes there were fewer, depending on how many had made their way to the stew pot of Sunday Dinner.

So going into the chicken house could be a real experience. There were all the chickens that got all riled up and started to flop their wings. With each flop a small cloud of chokingly dry chicken shit was lifted into the air, and I started to cough. Wet chicken shit seemed to find its way into every small crack in my bare fee. "Why that ain't no problem," said Uncle Shorty and Daddy. "That will just make you grow like the tomato vines."

Then there was the eggs themselves. Very often the eggs were clean and shiny brown, just the way they are supposed to be. But every once in while they would have chicken shit stuck to them with old straw mashed into the chicken doo. All of the eggs had to be washed in cold clean water. But when you found one with doo stuck to it, it was set side and washed last so that

I did not mess up the water.

I'd take the eggs into the house and Grandmother would put them in the refrigerator. I always thought that it was funny how she would put the new eggs near the back and move yesterday's eggs to the front.

Today, I laugh at myself, as I stand in front of the egg case at the Piggly Wiggly and open my carton of eggs. I look for cracks and not chicken shit.

Here is what you need:

Your cast iron egg-frying pan

A little lard or drippings from the little jar by the stove

Hunt up your eggs, salt & pepper.

Texas Pete hot sauce

Three or four popcorn kernels

Here is what you do:

1. I wash out the cast iron skillet in cold water with almost no detergent and wipe it dry. I want to remove dust, maybe, but not the pan's seasoning.
2. When the pan is dry I set it on the stove with a spoonful of drippings from the jar beside the stove and let the oil or lard come to almost smoking temperature, then set it on a cooler spot while I find other stuff.
3. Crack one or two or three or four eggs in a small bowl.
4. Put the cast iron skillet back on the hot stove and add in three or four popcorn kernels.

5. The second the popcorn pops, take it out and carefully pour your morning eggs into the pan. I always eat the popcorn — kind of an appetizer for breakfast.

6. Cover the eggs with black pepper and a little salt. Add a small amount of dill weed, too.

7. With a fork raise the edges of the egg and let some of the hot lard run up under it.

8. Now pick up the pan and slide the egg around while it cooks.

9. You can turn the heat off and let eggs cook to your preferred doneness. Me, I like my eggs just past the runny stage. I just do not like to chase the eggs across my plate.

10. Now just tilt the pan over the plate and let the eggs slide off onto it.

11. Inspect the cast iron skillet — notice there isn't anything in the pan. While it is hot, wipe it dry with a few paper towels.

Notes for the cook's eyes only:

- Read the pancake recipes.
- I like 7 or 8 strips of home-cured bacon.
- I like to put two drops of Texas Pete on each egg yellow.
- If there are no pancakes, then there ort to be three or four hot biscuits with lots of yellow cow butter, homemade jelly, or a small plastic bear of honey along with a full glass of cold sweet milk.
- Strong coffee is a requirement for a meal like this one.

Thicken Gravy or Gravy

Old habits are hard to break. Sometimes you just do things and don't even know you are doing them. For example, just the other day I was getting milk out of the refrigerator for a couple of my granddaughters. I took the plastic one-gallon container of 2% milk and shook it up and then smelled the milk before I filled their glasses. "Why did you do that?" they asked.

Well, when I was a kid we had whole fresh unpasteurized milk. When the milk set in the refrigerator for a while, a thick layer of cream would come to the top. You had to shake up the milk to mix the cream back into the rest of it. As for the smelling of milk, once in awhile the milk would sour. After a glass or two of soured milk, you quickly learned to smell it before you drank it.

You might be questioning where this is going. (PS, just between you and me, so am I, just a little.)

A few days ago I went to the garden and picked a five-gallon bucket full of fresh kale and turnip greens. I carefully washed each leaf and placed the greens in a two-gallon stew pot. I lit the outside eye on the grill and set them to boil while I went into the house for seasonings. I found the salt, pepper, garlic and Herbs of Provence. I reached over to the back of the stove for the small can of bacon drippings. I laughed all the way to the grill.

There has not been a small metal can on the back of the stove for collecting the leftover bacon, ham and sausage drippings in more than 30 years. But this day, for some reason, I reached for it. I think old habits and old memories are powerful things. I had to go back to the refrigerator and get out 8 strips of store-bought bacon to season my kale and turnip greens. When my five gallons of greens were cooked down, there wasn't more than a gallon of good fresh greens. My cousin Kevan stopped by and marveled at how good they smelled. All he said was, "Why aren't there eight or ten fresh potatoes boiling in them greens? That is the way I make them. What did you season them with?"

"I just used store-bought bacon." I know he was thinking about an old metal can on the back of his mother's stove.

I was once asked, "You say that you all had gravy at about every meal. You could not have fried ham or sausage all the time." Well, we did not eat meat for every meal, but we could have had gravy bread if Mamaw or Momma had wanted it and that is fact!

About every house I was ever in on River Ridge had a cook stove, either wood or an electric range. The one common thing was a grease cup, bowl or can setting on the shelf over the stove. Possibly this was true of all of Appalachia.

Every time Momma fried bacon, or ham or sausage she dumped the extra grease over into the grease jar. Momma had a jar that looked a lot like a flower pot with no hole. The grease level was always getting higher, but it never, ever got full. In the morning when Momma fried eggs she just dipped a spoonful or two over into the egg frying pan. If she was frying hamburgers, she would add a spoonful or two to the frying pan. The drippings always seemed to stretch the lard and that was very important on River Ridge, as was the health and hunger of little fat boys.

Another question people are always asking me is, "What is the difference between 'Thicken Gravy' and 'Gravy'?" The answer is simple to little boys on the River Ridge. Your gravy is the staff of life for country people, like me.

"Gravy" is just that—gravy with a given surname such as ham gravy, squirrel gravy, chicken gravy, or tomato gravy. You fry ham and you make ham gravy with grease. You spoon the extra grease over into the grease cup on the stove. Now when you walk down the steps in the morning or come in early from squirrel-hunting, you can smell the meat frying and you know what kind of gravy you are going to be eating. You learn the smells early on in life. Ham smells like ham; sausage smells like sausage, and salt-cured bacon smells like bacon. All of the extra greases are just put in the grease cup.

With all the adding and spooning out of the grease cup, the flavors get mixed up. Sometimes you just want gravy with your meal and for some reason there ain't no meat being fried. So Mamma just dips out five or six good-size spoonsful of grease from the grease cup and mixes it with flour and makes a pan of "Thicken Gravy."

Good stuff! It is a composite of all the wonderful stuff that has been dumped into the cup. But, "Thicken Gravy" does not have the same smell or tastes as a named gravy. Still, a growing boy has got to eat, and "Thicken Gravy" poured over cornbread or alongside fresh tomatoes is mighty good.

In these modern times nobody, not even me, keeps a grease cup on the back of the stove. Bacon drippings have gone the way of the Dodo Bird. We are taught that sausage grease, bacon grease and ham grease are not good for you to eat. But back in 1955, eating was important. We just did not have all the knowledge and knowhow that modern cooks have.

Today, in my house, we fry bacon or sausage and set it out of the pan on a paper towel to soak up the grease. The drippings are poured into a cup and carried to the backyard and dumped on the compost pile for the worms to eat. You know, I had a man tell me the worms we dug from the backyard were some of the most muscular worms he had ever seen. Through the years that grease has had the same effect on my muscular waistline.

Now my little granddaughters are into making and eating gravy. I love to watch them dig in and tell me how good it is.

Here is what you need:

1 deep cast iron Dutch oven

1 half gallon fresh milk

1 cup bacon drippings

1 cup flour

1 teaspoon black pepper

Salt – just have it on hand

Some warm water on hand, too

Just a little word here: you want your gravy to be thick. No one wants to go chasing the gravy across the plate. But the true thickness isn't known until the gravy cools, so start off carefully!

Here is what you do:

1. Dump the drippings into the Dutch oven and set it on the

stove.

2. Let the drippings come to a boil.
3. When the drippings are boiling, turn off the stove and dump the flour and pepper into the pan.
4. Stir the flour until the pan is cool.
5. Add the milk and keep on mixing. You might take a small taste and decide if you need some salt. If yes, go on and add it in now.
6. A note here: YOU MUST WORK VERY CAREFULLY, BECAUSE YOU JUST DON'T WANT ANY LUMPS! A child of River Ridge just might get his stomach caught up in a whorl if he ate lumpy gravy. Irritable bowl syndrome just might start off with lumpy gravy.
7. Set the Dutch oven back on the stove and slowly bring the heat up. KEEP an eye on the gravy; if you think it needs some water, add it now, not later.
8. Keep on stirring.
9. Once the gravy starts to boil, cut the heat down to simmer and just let all the goodness work together.
10. Don't let it stick. Sample a spoonful to see if it needs some salt, pepper or other spices.

Notes for the cook's eyes only:

- You truly can serve gravy with anything—I mean anything.
- I have set and watched "Duck Dynasty" on TV while eating a bowl of gravy.

- It is good on cornbread, hot biscuits, spread on a slice of light bread. It is a great complement to any meat dish I have ever eaten!
- Yes, it is that good.
- Any time you are making "chicken-fried steak," gravy ort to be made.

Grits

When I was a youngster there on River Ridge and down along the New River, we ate about anything. Most of the foods were great. Some were served because they were cheap. Once in awhile you could tell the turning of the calendar days by the foods served. As money got short, family foods became filling more than anything else. A lot of families were like this. But back in 1960, I thought that I was the only one—right there in River Ridge—experiencing a time when we ran out of money before we ran out of month.

During these times of money shortage we dug deep into the cellar and came out with cans of food stored away the summer before just for this situation. To supplement the canned tomatoes, there were jarred-up greens and wrinkled potatoes. We ate hominy grits and oatmeal, both cheap and filling. Daddy always said, "They will make a turd, so eat up."

As I got older, I just kind of swore off-n grits and oatmeal. Today, I know more about the world than I did back in 1960. For example, back in about 1985 I left my home on River Ridge—a suburb of Long Shop —for Martin, Tennessee. I drove all night, arriving New Year's Day 1985. Please don't ask me why, because I do not know. I think that I had it in my mind that there might be less traffic. Maybe I just needed a challenge or something. Anyway, I arrive in Martin, TN, about breakfast time. The only place in the whole county was a popular fast food restaurant. As soon as I saw the sign, I wanted a large cup of coffee and possibly three or four sausage biscuits. They did not have to have gravy either. I was just hungry.

I pull the long U-Haul truck back into the far corner of the parking lot and step out and stretch and slowly, gawkily lumber off to the restaurant. I am sleep-deprived and borderline grumpy. On the door hung a sign: "If the wait staff doesn't greet you within the first minute of sitting down, your meal is on us."

I take a seat. In less than one minute here comes the waiter. The young man looks to be about as sleepy as I am. Also, I think that he is on the verge of being a grump, too. I think that he also must have been up about all night. He says, "Good morning and Happy New Year!" Before I can even say a word, he sets down a large bowl containing at least one half gallon of something. The bowl is steaming hot with ¼ cup of butter melting in the middle and a large spoon sticking up on the side.

I inform the waiter, "Sir, I did not order that!"

"Oh I know sir. Them is your grits." He says. (Note: not grits, but 'them' grits.)

"Well, I still don't want grits for breakfast. I want sausage biscuits, some gravy and coffee," I answer back.

"Well sir, them is your grits," he answers.

We go back and forth two or three times discussing who owns the big bowl of grits. The waiter is getting upset, and I am getting mad. I finally say, "Just leave your grits on the table and bring me two sausage biscuits with gravy and a very large coffee."

He picks up my menu and turns to leave. I hear him say under his breath: "He acts like he don't want the grits. Them is his grits."

I soon learned that grits were part of every person's breakfast in West Tennessee. Everyone ate them. Before long, so did I. Every household had their own special way to fix them. Some ate them straight up, like the ones served to me on New Year's Day, while others were a little more interesting.

A few days ago, I stopped for dinner at a local restaurant here in Virginia. I ordered the pork chops and potatoes. When my dinner arrived the pork chop was cooked to perfection and the potatoes were great. They came in their own small bowl with a dollop of butter. But the most amazing part of the meal was the square patty of "Fried Grits." The next thing you know people will be talking about the world being round. Everything that comes around goes around.

Homemade Grits Squares

Here is what you need:

A saucepan

2 either cast iron or non-stick skillets (some extra vegetable oil)

A green glass mixing bowl, like the one used by Mother and Mamaw

1 cup water

½ cup milk (any % will do)

¼ Tablespoon salt

1/3 cup quick cooking grits

4 or 5 Tablespoons cheddar cheese

2 teaspoons of vegetable oil

2 or 3 Tablespoons onion chopped fine

1 tomato chopped

6 eggs

A small amount chopped dill (I like dill. You may not, so your own choice on the dill weed. But I think you ort to try it.)

½ teaspoon garlic powder

Black pepper to taste

Here is what you do:

1. In a saucepan, add the dry grits to cold water, milk and salt, and cook them until they are "grits." Stir them until they come to a very low boil and reduce the heat. Grits are a lot like gravy: they should be thick and have no lumps.

2. Stir in the cheddar cheese.

3. Once the cheese melts, dump the cooked grits out on a non-stick surface.

4. Just let the grits set until they are cool.

5. Heat up the first cast iron skillet or non-stick skillet, if you don't already have a cast iron one on the stove to heat up. Put a small amount of vegetable oil, lard or butter in the skillet so the grits don't stick. Take your time to make sure the skillet is up to cooking temperature. Grits will stick in a heart beat!

6. When the grits are good and stiff, cut them into 6 or 8 squares.

7. Carefully place the grit pieces in the skillet. Be careful not to let the squares touch. Cook on medium heat for about 4 or 5 minutes on each side. Slide them around some too. This does help keep them from sticking.

8. In the second cast iron skillet, add some vegetable oil. When hot, add the onions and cook until they are clear looking. Now add in the chopped tomato and cook for about 3 minutes.

9. In the mixing bowl combine the eggs, dry dill weed, black pepper, garlic powder and mix. Make scrambled eggs the way you like.

10. To serve, place a fried grit square on a plate, cover with scrambled eggs, top with onions and tomatoes.

Notes for the cook's eyes only:

- Miss Gail said she has never seen a person use as many pots and pans as I can. I guess I am just gifted at using up things! We do wash up a lot of dishes.
- It is a good idea to have a little extra cheddar cheese to top the grits. If in doubt, add more cheese.
- Again you cook the scrambled eggs the way you like them.
- Adjust the salt and pepper to your own taste.
- Try the dill. If you don't like it, try a sprig or two of rosemary or basil or thyme or. . .
- It is important to use a well-seasoned pan.
- About any seasonings or herbs work well with grits.

GROWING UP AND OUT ON GOOD FOOD

Tyler's Super Perfect Mashed Potatoes and Gravy

This year during the Thanksgiving Holiday I was the one treated to a great new family tradition. All the little girls, all five of them, were home for the holiday and each in her own way helped with the holiday meal. Tyler, the oldest, pitched in to make the mashed potatoes. I have to admit I have eaten a lot of mashed potatoes, but few could equal hers!

From the big metal bowl near the coffee pot we took ten or fifteen potatoes and put them in the sink to soak. She and I scrubbed them clean and then peeled them. That was about all I was asked to do. Miss Tyler cut the potatoes into small pieces and boiled them. After they had cooled a little, I spooned them into a colander to drain. Again, Miss Tyler took over.

She took an old potato-masher that was once her great-grandmother's and went to work. (This potato-masher was made by her great grandfather during World War II.) She mashed a little while and tasted a little while. "I think they need a little more garlic," she would say, and then turned the white potatoes kind of a light orange with garlic powder.

"Look at them. Don't you think they look a little dry?" In went another cup of heavy cream. "They are just missing something."

"Well, how about another small piece of butter?" I suggested.

Finally, “OK,” came the answer, while she added another whole stick of butter.

She left very small potato lumps throughout the potatoes. They had a wonderful taste—of potato, the right amount of garlic, the creamy texture of cream and the wonderful richness of butter.

For me, the best part was the little hands that made our Thanksgiving Mashed Potatoes.

A small side note. Tyler started eating the mashed potatoes and gravy as soon as they were deemed cooked and prepared to perfection. She called them her “super perfect mashed potatoes.” She carried a bowl with her while the remainder of the meal was being prepared. Where all the mashed potatoes and gravy went is a mystery to me. I guess she has a hollow leg.

Here is what you need:

15 right big white potatoes washed and peeled

1 large onion

A big stew pot

½ Tablespoon salt (or more)

½ teaspoon black pepper (or more)

½ Tablespoon garlic powder (or more)

A big glass bowl

2 cups heavy cream

2 sticks butter (You just never know if you might need it, but I will leave that up to you.)

Here is what you do:

1. Cut the potatoes into ½ inch cubes.
2. Put the cubed potatoes in a stock pot to boil.
3. Add one very finely chopped large white onion to the potatoes.
4. Add ½ Tablespoon of salt and boil.
5. Boil ONLY until fork tender, not mushy.
6. When you think they are done enough, remove from the heat and let set for a couple of minutes to cool off some.
7. Carefully spoon the potato cubes and onion into a real big green glass bowl.
8. Save the potato water for the gravy.
9. Taste a cube to see if more salt is needed; if yes, add to suit your taste.
10. Put in ½ teaspoon of black pepper.
11. Put in ½ Tablespoon of garlic powder.
12. Now mash the potatoes for just one minute—don't mash them into a potato paste.
13. Add in one cup heavy cream and one stick of butter and carefully fold in with a rubber spatula.
14. Taste a little, adjust: salt, pepper, butter, garlic and cream. Some choose to eat a ½ of a dish or so just to get things right.

Notes for the cook's eyes only:

- You want the potatoes to be thick enough to withstand having a gravy hole mashed in them on your plate. You don't want the gravy to start off running too quickly.

- Don't worry about the lumps; it just might help you out some if your gravy has a lump or two.

- If you want to make some simply different but dazzlingly flavorful mashed potatoes, use buttermilk rather than the traditional sweet milk. I promise you the end result will be good.

Rebecca's Cheesy Potatoes

There is just something about cheesy potatoes that will bring a Lytton to the dinner table. Or to the breakfast, lunch, snack and bedtime snack tables. My niece is a master of the cheesy potato.

When I was younger, my mother would make a recipe similar to this one. Mom baked thickly sliced potatoes in a Corning Ware dish, painted with lard to keep the potatoes from sticking. When they were done, she layered them into a second dish with longhorn cheese—a layer of potatoes and a layer of cheese; another layer of potatoes and a layer of cheese. She then browned the potatoes just before serving. You talk about something good.

Miss Rebecca, my niece, does her own cheese potatoes. They have won awards all over Long Shop at the Lytton Family Reunion.

Longhorn cheese was the yellow cheese that came from Mr. Tom Long's Store. It came in a 10- or 15-pound log. Mr. Long just cut off the amount you needed. Most people bought it by the inch. "Mr. Long, please cut me off about two inches of cheese," my mother would say. He then weighed your cheese purchase. Longhorn cheese was very good. We all liked it. I do not know if it was a cheddar or something else.

Here is what you need:

6 or 8 big Irish potatoes

1 full stick butter

A 12-ounce bag sharp cheddar cheese

A 16-ounce tub sour cream

Here is what you do:

1. Bake the potatoes in the microwave until fully cooked.
2. Slice the potatoes and layer them into a square casserole dish (9-inch).
3. Now melt the butter in the microwave and stir in cheese & sour cream.
4. Salt and pepper to taste.
5. Spread the butter, cheese and sour cream over the potatoes.
6. Cook in the microwave for five minutes.

Notes for the cook's eyes only:

- Be real careful with the potatoes and the microwave and don't get burned!!! They will tend to cook some after they come out of the oven.
- You can play with this recipe as much as you like. For example, I added onions to the mix. If you do this, cook the onions in the microwave first and mix them in when you do the cheese, butter and sour cream. It just works better.
- Add any fresh herbs you like in with the cheese.

The Zucchini

I cannot even spell zucchini without looking it up. I had not ever seen one of these things until I was probably 10 or 12 years old. It was late spring, and we were all working in the garden when Daddy announced, “Russell from work gave me this envelope of seeds. He said they were some new kind of squash. I think that I will plant them and see what happens.”

We dug up a place and made a few hills in the end of the garden by the barn. In no time the seeds sprouted and not much was said. When the zucchini flowered, everyone said that they were very pretty and there seemed to be a lot of flowers. In about a week there were lots of zucchini about the size of cucumbers. So we took about 20 of the little zucchinis home to eat. No one knew much about this vegetable.

We always cut cucumbers into small rounds and served them in a green bowl with lots of fresh onions and covered with vinegar. When you got ready to eat some, you forked out what you wanted and covered them with lots of salt and pepper. Sometimes green peppers were put in the vinegar bowl too. Oh, for a country boy, this is food direct from heaven.

So that’s what we did with the zucchinis. We kind of thought they were some kind of new cucumber. Holy macaroni, we soon learned that they were not! The onions were always good. The peppers were fine, but the new kind of cucumbers were just plan slick tasting. No one would eat them. “Them zucchinis just ain't ripe" was what we all thought on River Ridge. We just let them grow until they could ripen.

They grew to gigantic sizes. Some were as much as two feet long and 12 inches around. "Damn, that thing has got to be ripe," said Daddy. "It is growing so big that you can't help dragging the skin off-n the thing as it is drug across the ground." So we took another one home. Mother chopped up the zucchini and cooked it in the pressure cooker. It sure got done! When the pressure cooker cooled off, I was served a bowl full of light green slick gruel. It was just awful. No amount of salt or pepper could make it any better. We thought Mr. Russell had played a trick on us.

Daddy picked at least two wheelbarrows full of zucchini and rolled them over to the hog lot. There he chopped up each one with the corn cutter and called the hogs. The hogs rooted through the pile of chopped zucchini and turned up their noses and walked back down over the hill. "Damn, I ain't goin' to eat anything that a hog won't!" said Daddy. Them things just kept on flowering and plants just kept on growing.

After a while, some said them things are a green squash and you fry them just like a yellow squash. So we set to eating them. We learned the big ones—the ones that were about as big as a small boat—were just too big and tough to eat. The smaller ones were OK.

I thought we were the only ones experimenting with zucchini, but we were not. I just happened to be in Prices Fork picking up hay one afternoon and was asked to join a local family for a picnic supper out under the cool shade tree. One of the dishes served was "Stuffed Zucchini." The host was a recently married fellow, but since he had gotten married he had fell off to almost nothing. I think one of the reasons was them stuffed zucchini.

Stuffed Zucchini

Here is what you will need:

4 large zucchinis

2 or 3 yellow squash

2 healthy-sized green onions

4 large onions

1 green pepper

2 medium dead ripe tomatoes

½ teaspoon salt,

1 Tablespoon lemon pepper,

½ teaspoon rosemary,

1 Tablespoon garlic powder

A cup of Parmesan cheese from the green can

Here is what you do:

1. Cut the four big zucchinis in half lengthways and dig out the seeds.
2. Chop the yellow squash, green onion (tops and all), green pepper and tomatoes into ½- to ¼-inch pieces and dump the mixture into a large glass bowl.
3. Add the Parmesan cheese, salt, pepper, garlic powder and rosemary to the bowl and mix a few times.

4. Lay the zucchini boats in a baking pan (or pans) and fill the hollows with the mixture.

5. Put the dishes in the oven at 400^0 and bake for 30 minutes. Serve hot.

Notes for the cook's eyes only:

- I think you are going to need a summer salad to serve as a stomach filler.
- I like sweet tea, too.
- If possible, it is good to cook hamburgers on the grill with lots of Worchester sauce.
- The stuffed zucchinis were very good, and I liked them. But I think a country boy could starve to death with his stomach full. They are not packed with staying power. For a town boy, I think they would be ok.

Old Heat Stoves and Making Leather Britches

I sometimes wonder if old things can think and feel. For about as long as I have been working over on the mountain, these thoughts have puzzled me. Not long ago, I saw an old square metal box half-buried by brush and small rocks. I had myself half covered the metal box with grapevine cuttings. Every once in a while, I would pitch old tree limbs on top of the brush pile, too. With each pitch of brush, the metal box just seemed to hide deeper in the brush pile and crawl back into the recesses of my mind.

The old brush pile had grown and was getting to be an eyesore, so the first time there was an inch or two of snow on the ground, I wadded up a handful of newspapers and a few sticks and put a match to the papers. In just a few minutes, flames were jumping toward the sky. In less than an hour, the pile had been reduced to a thick mound of glowing red embers.

There in the middle of the embers sat the old square metal box. On closer examination I realized it was not a box at all, but a square wood heat stove that had not been damaged by the brushfire at all. It was an old chunk burner commonly used 75 to 100 years ago, and somehow seemed to be enjoying the heat. It had been resting on the brush pile for who knows how many years. Maybe it had been waiting for a night just like this one, for this was the first time in a long while the stove had been hot and dry. It seemed to glow in the heat.

I sat back in the warmth of the big fire and started to let my mind wander back to my own youth and all of the old woodstoves I had seen. Every fall, Daddy and I would wash our old woodstove with warm soapy water. Then Daddy would produce a big can of "stove black," and very slowly we would cover each and every surface of the old stove. We took out the draft regulators and removed all the rust and grit from the threads. We carefully cleaned out the firebox and replaced any broken firebricks. It looked might near brand new.

Our old stove was then set aside to wait for the first leaves to fall from the big white oak in the backyard. I was given to think that all wood stoves were treated this way.

When fall finally came, a fire was started. This fire would last until the warm days of spring. During these cold days, many a very large pot of water was left resting on top of the stove to add a little steam and moisture to the air in the house. "Free heat, so a feller better use it," everyone would say. Free my foot! I had to cut and carry that wood. It did not look like free heat to me. We also cooked a lot of food on top of the old wood heat stove to take advantage of this so-called "free heat." Free, I reckon, if you weren't the one always chopping the wood.

Long strings of "Leather Britches" (dried green beans) were one of the first things cooked. When it came time to cook the beans, five or six feet of the bean strings were broken off of the strings and dropped into a large stew pot and set by the stove for a few hours or overnight to warm up and rehydrate. After the breakfast dishes were cleaned up and set back on the sideboard, the "Leather Britches" stewpot was set on top of the heat stove. A large hunk of fat meat, cut in checkerboard pattern all the way from the salty front to the pig's skin on the back, was dropped into the water. Sometimes old wrinkly Irish potatoes were dropped in the bean water as well. There they would set all day, just simmering the day away. What a start to a great meal! That old stove may have cooked more than a thousand bowls of brown beans and hundreds of strings of Leather Britches.

As years passed, the old wood stoves were replaced with oil-burning furnaces and electric heat. Electric ranges became all the rage. Some of the old trusty wood stoves set idle for years. But some people still liked them.

Me, now I moved away for a few years, but one day I found my way back to River Ridge. When I felt the first cool breeze of fall, I started thinking about the old wood stove. Boys that grew up on River Ridge just need a wood stove. Chuck Shorter and my brother, Melvin, came to the rescue. The three of us just took a-holt of the old wood stove and brought it out of the basement of the house I grew up in and carried it into my basement. It may have weighed upwards of 800 pounds, but we were real men back then—the red-necked kind, and we knew it, too.

I think that old stove knew who we were. I washed it, again I painted it with stove black and replaced the broken fire bricks. When the chainsaw started up, life for the stove just started over!

Back to the brush pile. As the snow kept up falling and the mound of red coals hissed, the old wood stove just stood there by the rocks. I ain't for sure if it looked at me or maybe I was just reading its mind, but something kind of happened.

I began to think, "Wonder what happened to the old stove? Why was it thrown away and could not find a new home? Do you think that old wood stoves have some kind of feelings?" I just stood there knowing that this wood stove would never feel Leather Britches being cooked or pots of brown beans set on its large, smooth, cast iron top. Just maybe people don't need these things any more.

Often when I am leading a workshop, people will ask me questions. One of my favorites is: "Mr. Lytton, I know that you ate a lot of beans when you were growing up. But what in the world is 'Leather Britches'?" Well, back in the old days, say 1950 to 1960, people still grew very large gardens and green beans were part of every one of them. By the last of summer, pretty much every canning jar was full of tomatoes, brown beans, October beans and green beans. Very often there were one or two rows of beans still in the garden. You had to preserve them some kind of a way. Back then, we did not let foods go to waste. Those leftover rows of green beans were made into Leather Britches.

On River Ridge, on a very early fall Saturday, everyone gathered at Grandmother's house. Two or three big tables were set out by the big black willow trees. Early on in my life, I looked on these family gatherings as just another time to come together and fight gnats and mosquitoes. But on these particular days, we were going to make Leather Britches. First off, one person would go to the big garden and pull up one armful of green bean vines after another and carry them to the end of the tables. Then someone would pick up each vine, pick off all the beans and pitch them into a large white enamel dishpan. They'd then pitch the old vine over their heads so it would not be picked up again. They were fed to the milk cows.

Grandmother and two or three of my aunts would start the stringing. They would pick up each green bean and push a large sewing needle through the green bean pods. Attached to the needle was a very strong coarse thread. They created lengths of beans five or six feet long and carried them to Grandmother's back porch to hang up on nails to dry. The strings hung near the walls where the sun did not shine on them too much.

Often there were so many strings that walking the length of the back porch was hard. But a good path from door to door was kept open so one could make an unencumbered run to the toilet. Sometimes at night, you just don't have time to untangle yourself from the strings of Leather Britches. I think that is why they were eaten first.

By the time I was 8 or 10 years old, Leather Britches were not being made anymore. I think canned green beans at the Mick or Mack Grocery Store were considered better than all the work of growing, stringing and drying the beans.

As a side note, I can remember going to visit Grover Davis' family. They lived back in on the mountain near Wake Forest. On their front porch were long strings of green beans and yellow apples. Once they were dry, the strings were carried into the attic. I just loved the taste of dried apples. Many times, when I asked for more apples, Daddy told me not to eat any more, because they would swell up in me and my guts would explode and sling shit everywhere and "there is enough shit already being shot."

There is a group of our population who are trying to keep all of the old ways and practices alive. I have not seen one of these people make Leather Britches, but in year or two you will probably see old Leather Britches in some high-dollar natural food store.

Leather Britches

Here is what you need:

One 3-inch-by-3-inch piece of salt-cured fat meat cut in a checkerboard pattern. Cutting the fatback lets more of the goodness out into the water.

A large (2-gallon) stewpot with a lid

A white enamel dishpan

½ Tablespoon black pepper

Leather Britches beans: Break up the equivalent of 2/3 of the volume of the stew pot.

6 or 7 old potatoes cut into quarters (It might be a good time to use the last of the old cut potatoes.)

Here is what you do:

1. After supper, break the beans over the large dishpan. Some of the larger beans may be lost if you don't.
2. Rinse the dust off the beans, but do not soak them in this water.
3. Wash the potatoes.
4. Dump the Leather Britches and potatoes into the large stewpot, fill the pot to within one inch of the top and set it beside the wood heat stove for the beans to warm up and

rehydrate. Don't set the pot so close to the stove that the beans start to cook. Let the pot set there all night.

5. Come morning, check the level of water in the stewpot. Add the black pepper and the hunk of fatback. If the water level is low, refill to where there is about 2 inches of water over the beans.

6. Set the pot on a wood stove, and let it come to a very slow, low boil. The moisture in the house is good for everything.

7. Move the stewpot to a place on the heat stove where the Leather Britches can almost boil. Let then set there all day. The longer they set, the thicker the soup will get.

Notes for the cook's eyes only:

- The dry beans and wrinkly potatoes will drink up some water overnight. It is important to refill the pot before cooking.
- Salt? Well, some might be needed. You be the judge.
- Fatback. We always had plenty, so that is what we used. A piece of side meat, bacon, or ham hocks can also be excellent seasoning meats. Believe me, they are all good.
- Serving suggestion: Hot biscuits with apple butter, sweet milk, fried ham meat, a can of cold beets and fresh turnip greens are all good.
- Anything goes with well-cooked and seasoned "Leather Britches."

Julie's Pinto Bean Pie

I had not thought about a brown bean pie in at least 40 years. Miss Gail and I were in Napa Valley California visiting vineyards, and at this one high-end place, we were offered small samples of the winery/vineyard's finest foods to pair with their wines. One of the samples was a small plastic spoon of Bean Pie. I just kind of laughed under my breath. I never in my wildest imagination would have thought that place with chauffeured limousines and fancy sculptures on the lawn would offer me a sample of a simple food like a bean pie and a glass of chardonnay. Little fat boys from River Ridge may have a place in heaven after all.

If those people in Napa, California, can eat bean pies, so can I. They even gave us an index card with the recipe on it. Of course, I had lost it before I got to the car, so when I got to thinking about it, I went to a friend of mine, Miss Julie. She knows about everything there is to know about food and cooking and bean pies. Miss Julie has made bean pies and recommends this recipe.

Bean pies are not hard to make at all. Others tell me they are quite flavorful. I think they were a holdover from the Great Depression, when rural people had to make use of each and every scrap of food. As my father once said, "We ate anything that would make a turd." Now high-dollar people eat them because they taste good.

Here is what you need:

1 cup cooked pinto beans (cooked without seasoning)

1 cup white granulated sugar

3 eggs, beaten

1 teaspoon nutmeg

2 Tablespoons melted butter

1 unbaked pie shell

Here is what you do:

1. Set out the butter to get warm and then measure out 2 Tablespoons.
2. In a small bowl, beat the 3 eggs and set them aside.
3. Mash the beans well or run them through a food processor.
4. In a large, green glass bowl, mix the sugar and nutmeg.
5. Now add in the mashed-up beans and mix, but do not beat.
6. SLOWLY add in the eggs and mix.
7. Add the butter and mix.
8. Pour into the pie shell and bake at 350^0 for 45 to 50 minutes or until a toothpick comes out clean.

Notes for the cook's eyes only:

- Be careful not to beat the mixture to death. Too little mixing is better than too much mixing. Four of five good passes with a big wooden spoon may be enough.

- In the olden days Grandmother mashed the beans through an upright colander with a wooden paddle.
- Today, bean pies remind me of bean quiche.
- If it doesn't get thick enough, you might think about adding ¼ cup of self-rising flour to the sugar and nutmeg.
- I suggest you serve them with a romaine lettuce salad and mild dressing.

Greens a New Way

On River Ridge fresh greens was just part of everyday life and wasting food was just something you did not do, and that was all there was to it. So when you read this story be thinking about those two points: Greens and Waste. Sometime accidents aren't so bad, either. I also had a coworker inform me that I had a stomach made of iron and could eat about anything. Well, one afternoon I opened the refrigerator, and there were a whole lot of small containers of about everything; the trouble was there was not enough of anything to make a meal. There were lots of little jars and packages just about half full. So, I mixed them all together and ate it. I found it to be one fine meal, and I have tried replicating the meal many times and here is what I have come up with.

Here is what you need:

A small 8-ounce bag of fresh kale from the Piggly Wiggly, or just get it from the garden. Cut out the stems and throw them away. Cut the rest into ½-inch pieces

A small bag of fresh spinach again right from the Piggly Wiggly. Just cut the leaves into pieces the same size as the kale

1 small red onion sliced real thin

8 ounces drained kidney beans

8 ounces drained white beans—black beans work, too

1 shredded carrot

¼ small head of cabbage shredded (Once in awhile I will use red cabbage if I am feeding a guest, you know, just to add a little color to the meal.)

1 cup of blueberries—DON'T substitute blackberries; they mash up too easy.

¼ cup sunflower seeds or more if you like

8 or 9 cherry tomatoes cut in half

½ cup sweet and sour salad dressing

About 1 teaspoon of honey (It is hard to tell exactly how much with the little round wooden thing-of-a-bob used to get honey out of the jar.)

Here is what you do:

1. In a big metal bowl, add in all the greens, onion, beans, sunflower seed, blueberries, beans, carrots, and cabbage.
2. Mix all the vegetables around.
3. Pour the sweet and sour salad dressing into the bowl and mix again.
4. Add the honey last. Try to cover the top of the salad and again mix. (The sweet and sour taste are needed to offset the bitter taste of the kale.)
5. You can eat the salad now, but it's best to let it set in the refrigerator for a little while.

Notes for the cook's eyes only:

- At times I have added a few other things to this new kind of salad. I sometimes fry bacon crispy and brown then dry up all the fat. I crumble the bacon on top of the salad.
- I sometimes add in small pieces of mild cheese. I think that it again softens the taste of the kale.
- I have even eaten the salad with fried eggs on top. I think that this makes me more like one of those French chefs.

Creasy Greens

In the spring of the year my father, Elmer, wanted to make sure that my digestive system was thoroughly cleaned out and working real well before spring settled in for good. To accomplish this we often went to the Bell Farm and the Adams Farm. We would walk last year's cornfields and search the almost bare earth for "Creasy Greens." There were two kinds of wild greens growing in these fields. One was bitter, and you just did not want those, so we searched high and low for those creasy greens with the small leaves that grew flat against the ground. Early on, we would cut three or four Piggly Wiggly grocery bags full. As the days warmed up, the creasy greens got harder and harder to find. But we spent every Saturday in search of this River Ridge delicacy. Once in a while today, I find fresh creasy greens at the local Kroger store. They are never on the shelf any longer than a few minutes.

Here is what you need:

At least two grocery bags full of creasy greens washed thoroughly to get rid of the dirt and stuff.

A pound of so of salt-cured ham or lean side-meat fried and set aside.

6 or 7 green onions chopped up. If you don't have them, use just regular onions from out of the cellar.

½ cup vinegar

Some grease from the frying meat

Here is what you do:

1. Set the greens out on the counter so the water can drain out of them. You want them as dry as possible.
2. While the meat is cooking, run a big knife through the creasy greens, cut them into bite size pieces and dump them into a big mixing bowl.
3. Cover the creasy greens with a little black pepper.
4. Drain off almost all of the grease into the jar over by the stove.
5. When the meat pan is hot, dump the creasy greens into it and stir them around until they are wilted real good. DO NOT overcook the greens.
6. Dump the greens back into the big bowl and pour the vinegar over the top and mix a little. They are now ready to eat and enjoy!!

Notes for the cook's eyes only:

- Don't be surprised if you start with two big Piggly Wiggly bags of greens and end up with what would fill a ½ gallon jar.
- I like dried apple pies with my creasy greens.
- I would also suggest a tall glass of cold buttermilk. The cows are freshening, and there is plenty in the spring house.
- Fried potatoes are also welcome.

- Hot biscuits to put the fresh cooked ham on are almost a must.
- If you want, you can dip a little of the ham grease out of the jar and make a pan of “red-eye gravy.”

Okra

Yes, Okra. The year was 1968, and I can remember it like it was yesterday. Terry Albert and me had made a right big garden down by the crosstie cabin. We planted the normal vegetables: red and white potatoes, tomatoes, onions, green beans and lots of sweet corn. Somehow we came up with a bag of okra seed. Now we knew what okra was, but I had never eaten one little piece of okra before.

I had no clue when okra was ripe and ready to pick. But long about the first of August the okra was big; as big a roasting ear of corn. So I thought that if the roasting ears were ready so must the okra be. I took 20 or 25 okra pods to the house. Momma did not say much other than, "once in a while she would add okra to soup." Back in this time, Momma either fried foods or she used the pressure cooker. She looked the okra over and settled on the pressure cooker.

Momma took the big butcher knife and cut the 12-inch pod into one-inch pieces and dropped them into the pressure cooker. When she cut the okra pods it sounded like she was cutting baler twine. Yes, there were a lot of big strings and fibers running through this okra. She added a piece of salt pork and set the okra to boiling. Most foods cooked in the pressure cooker came out looking about the same: that is, very slick, very nondescript and cooked beyond recognition. But not the okra. It came out cooked down a might, but it had a totally different look about it. It looked right slick and was setting in a pan full of oily stuff.

Momma dished out a small bowl of okra for herself and quickly took a spoonful. She very quietly walked outside and spit two or three times. She then pitched her helping of okra over the fence into Mr. Luther's field. She walked back into the house and drank down a tall glass of water. She kind of swished it around some before swallowed. She then looked at me, "Well, let me get you a dish of okra." She put the bowl down in front of me and asked, "What do you think?"

I took a big spoonful and tried to swallow, but before I could swallow it had slipped down my gullet. With eyes real big, I took another spoonful, but this time I was ready for the stewed okra. I kept my teeth shut so it would not go down so quickly. What I experienced was an example of pure awful. I ran out the door like Momma had and spit two or three times real hard. It took a cup of hot back coffee to clean off my tongue.

I do not think that I had experienced anything so slick and lumpy ever before. Except maybe having a real bad cold. Momma just started to laugh. She asked me, "What are we going to do with this stewed okra? Feed it to the hogs?" We both looked at each other and questioned, "Do you reckon the hogs will eat this?"

Momma had stepped out of the room and about this time my younger brother came through the door. I told him that Mother had made stewed okra, and it was one of her favorite foods from her childhood. I showed him my bowl and said, "This stuff is awful, but somehow I ate it. So please eat it and like it."

Well, Momma gave my brother a dish, and I must say I was proud of him. He ate three spoonsful before he bolted for the door. He hung on the catalpa tree and spit and gagged and spit some more. I will not tell you how he described the slick lumps in the stewed okra. No, I am not protecting your eyes and ears; I am trying to protect my stomach!

Okra – West Tennessee Style

When I moved to West Tennessee about everyone ate okra. I almost moved back to the hills when I heard "everyone ate okra." All I could think of was: "Where in the world have I come this time?"

Here is what you need:

One big cast iron skillet

20 small okra pods no more than 1 inch long

1 real big onion cut into small ½-inch cubes

2 or 3 Tablespoons lard, bacon drippings or Crisco

Salt, black pepper

Some red pepper, too, if you like it

Here is what you do:

1. Put the lard in the skillet and set it on the stove to get hot.
2. When the lard is bubbling hot, add in the okra and onions.
3. Cook the mixture until the okra is tender and the onions are starting to get uniformly brown.
4. Once in awhile some of the West Tennessee people would mix a tablespoon of all-purpose flour into the mixing bowl with onions and okra, just enough to evenly coat each piece,

and then fry. Both ways have their own character and both are good,

Notes for the cook's eyes only:

- In West Tennessee we ate fried okra with purple hull peas, lots of sweet milk, cooked greens and berry pies.
- Okra and stewed tomatoes are good, too. If you want, you can dip a little of the ham grease out of the jar and make a pan of "red-eye gravy."

Corn Pudding

I do think that one of the reasons that I have such a manly appearance is because of corn pudding! That is because I ate the same stuff that we fed to the hogs as they fattened for slaughter. CORN! We used a blender to mush up the corn that was a little past eating and starting to get hard—corn that could very easily have been fed to the hogs!

I have heard speakers talk about the importance of corn to the inhabitants of the Appalachian Mountains. It wasn't until I was much older that I learned that I was nothing more than an inhabitant. For years, I thought that I was just like every other little boy. Well anyway, Uncle Shorty loved to soak the corn kernels in wood ash and make hominy. It was OK. Grandmother would dry the hominy over the wood stove and grind it up to make "hominy grits." Often they tasted a little like coffee and had a few coffee grounds floating in them. She never made more than a little bit. I think it was just something to do.

Yes, the sweet corn was roasted in the shucks. We just had to have cornbread. In the early summer we would even make spoon bread out of the roasting ears that were starting to get hard. Sweet and good!

Back then, I think my favorite way to eat corn was in corn pudding. At early family reunions there were always two or three different recipes of corn pudding. Grandmother always served hers in a dish that looked just like a giant ear of corn. I sometimes see the old corn dishes at high-dollar antique shops. I look, but I never do buy one. I do, though, think back to the days of Grandmother's Corn Pudding.

Here is what you need:

3 Tablespoons butter—go on and rub a thick even layer of it all over the inside of the pan.

3 cups corn—you can cut it off the cob, use thawed out frozen corn or canned corn. Or you can get a jar from the cellar.

Dump the corn in the bowl and stir the kernels just to make sure none of them are stuck together.

5 eggs—fresh brown ones are the best, I think.

1 cup cold heavy cream for whipping

2 Tablespoons sugar

¾ cup milk

4 Tablespoons warm butter

3 Tablespoons all-purpose flour

2 teaspoons baking powder

1 teaspoon salt

Here is what you do:

1. Cut the oven on to 350^0 .
2. If you haven't already buttered the baking dish do it now. You will need one at least 8 x 8 x 2. One just a little bigger

or deeper might be better.

3. Take out one cup of corn and dump all the rest of the ingredients into a food processor. Mix until almost smooth, then add in the one cup of whole corn. Don't chop the whole kernels up. In the old days Mother would run the corn through a hand-cranked sausage grinder. Believe me, the food processor is a much better idea!
4. The cream will puff up a bit. That is ok.
5. Now dump the corn mixture into the waiting buttered dish and bake for 45 minutes or until the center is solid. You can stick a broom straw in the center. If it comes out clean, the pudding is done.
6. Let the corn pudding cool before serving.

Notes for the cook's eyes only:

- I like corn pudding served both cold and hot. When it is served cold, I think a big spoonful of whipped cream is a good idea.
- Some of the time people add more sugar—you decide what you prefer.
- I like tomatoes, dumplings, pinto beans, chicken-fried beefsteak, gravy and hot butter biscuits with my corn pudding.
- Corn pudding can be dressed up real nice if company or the preacher is coming over to eat with the family.
- I cannot remember if Grandmother baked her corn pudding in the big ear of corn dish or just spooned it over into the dish for serving. Memories are a strange thing, aren't they?

Corn and Green Pepper Salad

Not too long ago I had the privilege of setting down to eat at one of the finer homes in the area. I just thought that I was fix-n to have a great meal. When the table was set the cook said, "Just the other day I saw this new recipe on the TV and thought that I would try it. It is really good."

I got me a really big spoonful, and you guessed it. Now that is not what I was thinking. I was thinking that I ort to get me a job as one of those TV cooks. "Well, no, not really," I was thinking.

I just thought back to corn and green pepper salad. It was another way of saying summer. As I have said over and over, on River Ridge there were about 12 to 15 foods that we ate on a regular basis. Peppers and corn were part of this group in the summer. So mothers were always searching for different ways to fix foods. By the time "Corn and Pepper Salad" appeared I was just about full of roasting ears and stuffed peppers. I loved both vegetables, but enough is enough. So when the salad appeared, I dug in and liked it.

But to town people I reckon it is something new. Something that they discovered on TV.

Here is what you need:

1 quart canned corn from the cellar, drained dry

1 big onion—chopped fine, top and all. You want the green for color.

1 large green pepper

1 red pepper if you have it

1 red or pink tomato chopped into small pieces and set in a tea strainer to drain out some juice

1 cucumber, not peeled and cut into pieces no bigger than a kernel of corn

¼ teaspoon black pepper

¼ teaspoon salt

¼ teaspoon garlic powder, or if you wish you can chop two garlic cloves

A large green glass bowl

1/3 cup of Italian salad dressing (In the old days Grandmother and Mom used apple cider vinegar and some salt. Today, I use Italian salad dressing.)

Here is what you do:

1. Hunt up a medium-sized glass bowl with a lid.
2. Dump everything into the big green bowl and mix it around.
3. Pour the salad dressing over the mixture.
4. Eat a few spoonsful and adjust the salt, pepper and garlic.
5. Today, I use a lot of herbs. I chop coarsely 5 or 6 sprigs of sage, rosemary, thyme, chives and flat parsley plus any other thing I have.

6. Dump the corn salad into a dish with a lid and put it in the refrigerator for a few hours.

Notes for the cook's eyes only:

- You can adjust this recipe any way you like, such as adding more vegetables.
- Corn is real forgiving. There is no way to mess up corn salad.

Cabbage as Made on River Ridge

I once read that in 1900 Americans ate more than 50 pounds of cabbage per person per year. Today, I bet we Americans do not eat more than 10 pounds per person. Except on River Ridge; we still hold on to the 50 pounds per year. Me, I am more of 60-pound person. All of the Lytton-DeHart cross clan eats cabbage. We ate cabbage fried, boilt, and chopped with hot dogs. You think it up, we ate it. But my two favorite ways to eat cabbage are as coleslaw and steamed.

Coleslaw

Here is what you need:

1 large head fresh green cabbage

1 very small head red cabbage

1 medium carrot

1 very small onion (You may even want ½ of a small onion. Let your taste be the guide.)

1 cup mayonnaise

½ teaspoon mustard

½ teaspoon black pepper

½ teaspoon salt

¼ teaspoon dill seeds

¼ teaspoon caraway seeds

Just a shake of olive oil

1 Tablespoon paprika

Here is what you do:

1. I place my grater inside a large metal bowl and grate the whole head of green cabbage. While it's there, I grate the red cabbage and carrot, too.
2. Scrape off the cabbage from the grate with a spatula—NOT YOUR FINGER.
3. Finely chop the onion and add it to the cabbage bowl.
4. Stir the cabbage with a spatula until the green cabbage, red cabbage, onion and carrot are evenly mixed.
5. I like to shake the olive oil over the cabbage. This will make the herbs stick to it.
6. Sprinkle on the dill seeds, caraway seeds, black pepper and salt.
7. In a small bowl mix the mayonnaise and the mustard then fold it into the cabbage.
8. Put a cover on the dish and put it in the refrigerator for a few hours before serving.

Notes for the cook's eyes only:

- After you have made a bowl or two, you can start playing with herbs.

- The red cabbage is needed for color and taste.
- Mayonnaise and traveling to a family reunion: MAYO DOES NOT TRAVEL WELL.
- There must be a thousand ways to enjoy coleslaw.

Steamed Cabbage and Fresh Herbs

Here is what you need:

1 (one) medium head cabbage cut into small wedges

A double boiler

4 Tablespoons melted butter

A few sprigs each fresh parsley, rosemary, thyme and sage

ç teaspoon black pepper

¼ teaspoon garlic

¼ cup Parmesan cheese

Here is what you do:

1. Carefully place the cabbage wedges in the double boiler.
2. Steam until tender but not over-cooked.
3. Chop up the herbs about as small as you can. If you want, you can put them in one of them real small chopper/ blenders with butter.
4. No matter how you cut them up, I like to mix the warm butter and herbs together. Mix in the garlic, too. Put the herb, garlic and butter mixture in the refrigerator.

5. When the cabbage is tender, possibly with a little crunch left in it, take it off the stove and set it off the boiling water.

6. Place a wedge on each guest's plate.

7. Carefully spread the herb-butter-garlic mixture on the hot cabbage and sprinkle with Parmesan cheese right from the can.

Notes for the cook's eyes only:

- Try to time the cooking of the cabbage to the time you are going to serve dinner.

- Cabbage can be right sweet-tasting, too.

Charles' Balsamic Onions

In the modern times people do not eat onions as vegetables on their plate. Well, I know an onion is a vegetable, but what I am saying is onions are a lot like cabbage: people don't fix them and eat them the way they once did.

When I was a child growing up on River Ridge, onions were a part of almost every meal. We ate them raw with a little salt right out of the garden. Almost every dish from turkey to mutton had onions as an ingredient. Sometimes fried onions or baked onions were the second vegetable on your plate.

Even in these more modern times, I still slowly fry onions in butter with a little salt and black pepper and serve them with steak and baked potatoes. They are still very good.

As times have changed, so have I. When we are having guests over, I like to make my balsamic onions. I like to cook them outside on the grill. The smell fills the whole neighborhood. Give them a try, and see if you don't agree with me! They are very good.

Here is what you need:

8 small white onions cut into quarters (Cut off the tops and slice into quarters ensuring that each quarter is connected still by its root.)

1 cup Balsamic vinegar

1 small handful fresh tarragon from the herb garden

2 Tablespoons crushed garlic or six or eight cloves

2 Tablespoons olive oil

¼ teaspoon salt

½ teaspoon black pepper

A large glass bowl, something that will hold at least two quarts

A big cast iron skillet

Here is what you do:

1. In a two-quart glass measuring bowl, mix all the herbs, vinegar and garlic.

2. Add in the onions and stir. Be careful not to separate the onion quarters so that they will not stick together.

3. Let the onions marinate for about four hours in the refrigerator in a covered container.

4. Every time you walk past the refrigerator, carefully turn the onions and reseal the container.

5. When the pork loin goes on the grill, so do the onions.

6. I place the cast iron skillet on the grill with the pork loin. I then dump the onions, herbs, and vinegar into the pan.

7. I want the onions to cook slowly. I just want the fluids to reduce down into a very thick juice. If this takes two or three hours, that is fine with me. Just cook the onions slowly.

Notes for the cook's eyes only:

- I think the Balsamic Onions make a great side dish for any meat dish.
- I like to cook them down until they are very think and the acidity of the vinegar is greatly reduced.
- They sure do make a great complement to pork dishes.
- Don't forget pinto beans, coleslaw, and green beans, too.
- When cooking take care to have a small piece of the root connected to each section. It does help to hold the onion wedge together.
- I have used apple cider vinegar, and the onions just taste as good.

Charles' Summer Cabbage

I just love cabbage. I think it is one of the most overlooked vegetables in the world. It is versatile and very easy to prepare in many ways. Cabbage just screams out for fresh herbs. At least I can hear it; I hope you can too.

I told you we ate a lot of cabbage!

Here is what you will need:

1 medium head green cabbage, cut into eight even pieces. Cut the head in half then into quarters leaving a small piece of the stalk on each of the eight pieces. This will keep the pieces together.

3 to 4 sprigs fresh rosemary

8 or 10 6-inch sprigs fresh chives

5 sprigs tarragon

5 to 6 sprigs flat parsley

5 Tablespoons olive oil (When no one is looking I use YELLOW COW BUTTER!)

A pinch both salt and pepper

Small blender or chopper

A double boiler

Here is what you do:

1. Wash and clean the herbs. If you choose to use butter, and I hope you do, let it come to room temperature in a small glass measuring cup while the herbs dry on a paper towel.

2. Just before you have to take the pork loin off the grill to rest, start the water boiling in the lower half of your double boiler. While the water is heating up, carefully arrange the cabbage slices in the top half of the double boiler. Be careful not to break the sections. Once the water is boiling, place the top half of the double boiler over the hot water.

3. Put all the herbs in the chopper. Do not add the butter. Chop everything until each piece of the herb plant is finely chopped. Don't chop the herbs into a green slurry.

4. Clean the herbs from the chopper and mix with the warm butter. Stir until they are evenly mixed.

5. Do not steam the cabbage too long. Only cook until it is tender and keeps its nice light green color. I like to eat my cabbage when it still has a soft crunch.

Notes for the cook's eyes only:

- When it comes time to serve the meal, I like to place two pieces of pork loin on the plate and spoon on two teaspoons of peach marmalade and soy sauce. I then place a wedge of cabbage across the pork loin and spoon on the butter herb sauce. I cover the entire surface of the cabbage wedge.

- I then add a few spoons of balsamic onion.

- If the plate doesn't have enough color, you can add a hunk of French bread. I have also added a slice of red tomato and a slice of yellow tomato.

Glazed Sweet Potatoes that Weren't Sweet Potatoes

When I was younger, we only ate sweet potatoes in the fall. Daddy said that we had too much clay and too many rocks in our River Ridge soil to grow good sweet potatoes. Instead, we bought them from the Rawleigh Salve man. But we still had Glazed Sweet Potatoes anyway. When I got to be about eight or nine years old, I learned that when the sweet potatoes ran out, Mother would fix carrots. I was eating Glazed Carrots and thought they were Glazed Sweet Potatoes. She never said any different, and I never saw a need to ask. I always ate what Mother put on the table and liked it. I learned early to be thankful for whatever food was on my plate. That is except for the stewed okra. Thankfulness just ran out on the stewed okra.

We could grow good carrots. But getting them out of the ground was a problem! You had to take a round pointed shovel with you to the garden to dig the carrots. The ground was so hard that carrot tops would break off when you were trying to pull one. You had to pull real hard, if you did get the carrot loose from the ground, it just might fly back and hit you on the head and knock you out colder than a watermelon resting in the cellar.

I was always worried about straining my back trying to pull them rascals up. But in just a few minutes you could always dig up all you needed with a round pointed shovel.

Here is what you need:

15 good-size carrots

½ pound yellow cow butter

5 Tablespoons dark brown sugar

½ teaspoon salt

1 Tablespoon lemon juice

A good-size saucepan

Here is what you do:

1. Wash and peel the carrots and cut them into ¾-inch slices.
2. Boil until they are just about tender.
3. Drain off all the water, and let stand for a few seconds to dry off some and cool.
4. Add the cow butter, brown sugar, and lemon juice.
5. Set the pan back on the stove and stir very slowly.
6. Make sure the glaze touches each piece of carrot. Be careful not to mush them up.
7. Dump into a bowl and serve. (Use an old green glass bowl if you have it.)

Notes for the cook's eyes only:

- I like to always have brown beans with carrots. Early green beans were always welcome along with cornbread.
- We did not serve any meat with these meals.
- Cold sweet milk is a fine drink.
- P.S., glazed carrots are as good as sweet potatoes.

Sweet Potatoes

Every fall Momma and Daddy would order a large box of sweet potatoes from the Rawleigh's Salve man. We ate sweet potatoes cooked every way I can think of, but Mamma Ruth just loved to have them made into a Sweet Potato Soup. Here is how I make it today.

Sweet Potato Soup

Here is what you need:

6 whole sweet potatoes

8 or 10 strips bacon fried crispy

2 Tablespoons olive oil

2 medium white onions cut into ½ cubes

Salt to taste

½ cup brown sugar

1 cup half and half

1 cup cream (I sometimes just use milk, but cream makes the soup smoother.)

4 cups chicken stock

One cup good quality white wine. I like to use steel-aged Chardonnay, because there is no oak flavor. Pinot Gris or any other will do.

Now here is what you do:

1. First off, I like to bake the sweet potatoes in a large cast iron skillet. I just cook them until they are soft and done.

2. When they are cool, pull off the skins and chop up or mash the potatoes.

3. In that cast iron skillet now put the olive oil, the onions, salt, pepper and wine and butter. Cook for a while on medium heat. I like for the content to reduce by half.

4. Now add the chicken stock, half and half, cream, brown sugar and bring to a boil. Once the pan is boiling reduce the heat to low.

5. Sometimes I now add in the bacon crumbles. Other times I hold off and add them after I run the soup through the food blender.

6. Once you think the soup has cooked together, take it off the stove and let it cool down. When you can safely handle the liquid run it through the food processor. You want the soup to be thick and creamy.

Notes for the cook's eyes only:

- I like to have a large double boiler for foods with milk and cream. If you don't, just remember milk and cream will stick, so cook slowly and stir often.

- If you like your soup thicker, take the lid off when it is boiling to allow it to reduce more.

- I like to eat my sweet potato soup with a big spoonful of sour cream setting on top.
- I always prefer to eat mine with fried chicken, coleslaw and cornbread.
- I sometimes eat it kind of like a dessert with coffee.
- Not long ago I served sweet potato soup as a side dish with hot chili, and it was very good. You go on and eat it any way you like.

Potato Salad

Here is another food that I just do not eat much anymore. Not that I don't like it, I guess I just had my fill. I think it is a lot like pumpkin is for my brother Melvin; he just doesn't like them anymore. We ate a lot of potato salad when we were kids. Potatoes were served at about every meal in one way or another. Potato salad was a Saturday or Sunday meal. Mostly I think of it as Sunday afternoon food: something that you serve with fried chicken, pinto beans and buttermilk.

Truly, potato salad was a staple of the River Ridge table. It was fixed lots of ways just to add a little different flavor and variety. Once in a while someone would make a dish of potato salad and not peel the potatoes all the way. Usually, this was done in the early summer with new red potatoes. Now that was good.

One thing for sure, we always had potatoes and onions in the zinc bucket by the door! Eggs were in every refrigerator right beside the crock of cream.

Here is one funny note. If Daddy did not see the red pepper can he would eat the potato salad. If he did see the can he'd holler that it was too hot for his liking. "Ruth what in the world are you trying to do to me? Damn them is hot!" Daddy would say.

I have one family member who would turn into a wild person if he ate mayonnaise, so he could not see the jar. If they did not know all the ingredients, both he and Dad would eat and enjoy. Sometimes Mother told them and they passed on the potato salad.

Here is what you need:

A real large green glass bowl

10 potatoes from the mound out in the edge of the garden.

1 cup chopped sweet pickles

1 cup black olives cut into ¼'s

1 Tablespoon garlic power

1 teaspoon salt

1 teaspoon black pepper

½ teaspoon cayenne pepper

4 boiled eggs cut into large pieces

2 stalks celery chopped—chop the leaves too

1 or 2 medium onions chopped real fine (I like to use red onions for the color.)

½ cup cold cream

2 cups mayonnaise

¼ cup yellow mustard

Some like a little lemon juice.

Here is what you do:

1. Go on and get everything found.

2. Wash and peel the potatoes. If they are a little wilted, put them in cold water for an hour or two to swell back up.

3. Cut the potatoes into 1-inch cubes and boil them until they are just fork tender.

4. Drain them in a colander until dry, and dump them into the big green glass bowl. Save the potato water for gravy.

5. Carefully sprinkle the salt, red pepper, black pepper and garlic powder evenly over the boiled potatoes.

6. Give the potatoes three or four slow turns with a big wooden spoon, trying not to mash them.

7. Add the cream, olives, mayonnaise, mustard, onion, celery, boiled eggs, and lemon juice if you are using it.

8. Again carefully stir the mixture.

9. Put a lid on the bowl and put it in the refrigerator until you are ready to serve.

Notes for the cook's eyes only:

- If you wish, you can mix the herbs and spices in a small bowl, then add them at one time.
- Today, you can add all kinds of fresh herbs to the recipe.
- Some may choose to place all the other ingredients in another bowl and mix them up; then add them to the potatoes all at one time.
- On River Ridge, the focus was on putting the potato salad on the table more than the way it was fixed. My way is quicker, and somehow it works.

- If this recipe is a little too wet for your taste, make a note and drop back on the cream a little the next time.
- Some may not like the 2 cups of mayonnaise, but I do.
- Please consider pinto beans, chow chow, butter, hot biscuits, coleslaw and sweet tea. This matches up well with the history of River Ridge. If this is going to be Sunday dinner and Grandmother has been out in the chicken lot chopping off chicken heads, you know fried chicken is on the menu, so take the potato water and make thick white milk gravy
- Please note that there are at least one thousand ways to make potato salad. This is just a starting place for you.

Parsnips and Turnips

I find it so funny to look in a high-dollar cooking magazine and see an advertisement or recipe for cooked parsnips and turnips. During my childhood, parsnips and turnips were part of every fall. We ate them a lot, so much so that today I rarely eat a cooked turnip and almost never eat a parsnip. I plant a lot of turnips every fall, though. I just love the greens, and I find no finer place than to set up on the hill next to the garden and eat the fresh, right-out-of-the-garden raw turnips. I just wipe them off on the tail of my shirt, lick a spot and add salt. No better food anywhere! Cooked turnips? Well, they are OK. They will keep you alive I guess.

One afternoon when I was working in West Tennessee, an older man walked up to me in the garden as I was preparing the ground to plant turnips. This was Mr. R. O. Woolwine. People around just called him "Mr. Row." He inquired about what I was doing, and I explained how much I like turnip greens and I wanted to get a few seeds in the ground before that first set of September rains started.

He exploded. "Damn, expletive, expletive, I ain't planting no turnips, and I ain't ever eatin' another one either! Back during the Depression my daddy worked chopping a winter's worth of wood for a man. His pay was a horse-drawn wagon of turnips. That winter we ate raw turnips, fried turnips, turnip stew. Mom would put whatever salt-cured meat we had or she could find in the turnip pot, so we all could get a little of the goodness out of the meat. Late spring we moved to another farm, and we loaded up the last of the turnips and carried them there. No sir, I ain't eatin no more turnips—go hungry first."

Well, I am not turned off by turnips the way Mr. Row was, but I ate enough of them to know where Mr. Row was coming from.

As for the parsnip part of the story, Grandmother would often serve turnips and parsnips at the same meal. Sometimes she would cook them together, just to put something different on the table. Sometimes she would boil the turnips and fry the parsnips. This was my favorite way to eat them both. Put a little yellow cow butter, black pepper and salt on the turnips, and they are just fine.

One time, a lot of the cousins and my family were gathered around Grandmother's dining room table. You guessed it: there was a dish of boiled turnips, mashed like potatoes and just swimming in yellow butter. Just off to the side was a platter of fried parsnips. They were cut down the middle and looked like a long triangle. Think about the shape of a carrot if you were to cut it down the middle from the top to the bottom. They had been rolled in flour and fried in hot lard. They were golden brown, too! When you cut into them, they had a light yellow color on the inside. One of my little cousins said, "Oh no, Mamaw, not parsnips again!"

Mamaw answered back, "No honey, one of your uncles has been to the river. That there is coon tail perch all fried up golden brown; just look how the frying even colored up the meat on the inside."

A few years later we had fried parsnips for supper one night and I asked Mother, "Now, you ain't going tell me that this is a fried fish are you?"

"No it is just a parsnip. Keep in mind that back then your Mamaw had one thing on her mind—keeping you all fed. If it took a little white lie to pull that off, it was OK."

Back then, about 1960, we had a lot more to eat than turnips and parsnips, but Mamaw still had World War II and the Depression fresh in her mind, and with ten children she had to make each turnip and parsnip count. So, we still ate the turnips and parsnips.

Don't go looking down on turnips and parsnips. In real high-dollar restaurants, you will find these root vegetables on the menu. They are kind of like hominy grits to me. I like a little piece of the past. But to this current generation, turnips and parsnips are brand new foods that they have just discovered.

Boilt Turnips

Here is what you need:

A two-gallon stock pot

10 or 12 good-size turnips washed, peeled and cut into quarters

2 Tablespoons salt

1 Tablespoon pepper

A block of yellow cow butter, one with a large four-leaf clover molded into the top

Here is what you do:

1. Wash, peel and quarter the turnips.
2. Place each piece into the stock pot and add the salt and pepper.

3. Cover the turnips with water. I like to see them covered by about 1 ½ inches of cold water.

4. Boil the turnips until they are fork tender.

5. The second they are tender, they are done!

6. Dump the turnips into a colander. No, there is no need to save the turnip water for making gravy. No, don't save the water!

7. Put the turnips into a green glass bowl and add a few chunks of yellow cow butter. Taste one or two, and see if they still need a little salt and pepper.

8. Put them on the table hot!

Notes for the cook's eyes only:

- Do not over boil the turnips; they can turn into a watery mush.
- Drain the turnips real good.
- You want the hot turnips swimming in butter
- I like for my turnips to come to the table with a thin uniform layer of black pepper. I kind of like a small handful of fresh herbs chopped up, too. I often set the herbs beside the green glass bowl of turnips so eaters can get what they want.
- Turnips can also be boilt with potatoes.
- Fried turnips are good, too, especially if they are cooked with onions.
- Once in a while, Mother would mash one turnip in the mashed potatoes. It adds a whole different flavor.

Fried Parsnips

About the only way I ever ate a parsnip was fried. We grew a short row of parsnips each year. The parsnips were planted in the spring after the last frost date and left in the garden until up in late summer or early fall. They were dug about the time we dug potatoes. Parsnips were buried in the dirt mound with the cabbage. If you put them in the potato bin cellar they tended to wrinkle up a lot. We had big family, and a bushel of parsnips was all we needed.

Here is what you need:

A large cast iron skillet

A cup or so of good lard.

8 or 10 parsnips taken from the buried vegetable dirt pile, washed and peeled.

Cut the parsnips lengthwise. Do not cut them into little rounds.

If the parsnips are a little limber and wrinkly, set them in cold water for a while to get them tufted up again.

1 Tablespoon salt and 1 Tablespoon pepper, or to your taste

Here is what you do:

1. Put a Tablespoon or two of lard in the cast iron skillet and let it get good and hot.
2. When the lard is about to start thinking about smoking, slowly add the parsnips to the skillet.
3. You want to turn the parsnips over just one time, so nudge them around a little with a fork some so they don't stick.
4. Cook them for about five minutes on one side and then turn them over and cook for another five minutes.
5. When they are brown on both sides take them out and set them on a paper towel for a minute, but serve them hot!

Notes for the cook's eyes only:

- It is important to use hot lard. If you don't, the parsnips can get soggy and greasy.
- I have seen parsnips dipped in an egg wash and rolled in flour then fried. I bet they would be good that way.
- I bet you could slice them like a cucumber and fry them. I have not eaten them this way, but I think it would work.
- This goes along with the topic of rediscovering foods. I have not seen a cooked parsnip in a restaurant in like forever. A few nights ago, I went to a high-dollar restaurant and ordered the pork chop and mashed potatoes. Yep, parsnips had been mashed into the potatoes. It was great. Something old made into something new.

ONLY AN APPALAYCHUN WOULD SAY TOMAHTO

(APPALACHIANS KNOW BETTER)

Chuck's Story about Elmer's Thermometer

As this story starts, it is 10^0 outside, and I have been thinking about Chuck Shorter, not the wind or the snow. I can bet that at least once this day Chuck has thought about my father, Elmer, and the thermometer that once hung on the old locust tree outside the kitchen door.

It was always hotter and colder there under the locust tree than any other place on Planet Earth. Daddy had an old metal R.C. Cola thermometer nailed on the big tree to record the official temperature for River Ridge, which was relevant for the whole world.

This old R.C. thermometer had a small slender glass tube of red alcohol, just like all thermometers of my day. This little tube was held in place by two very small metal clamps that kept it in alignment with the numbers so it could inform you of the current temperature. When the wind blew, the old metal thermometer would shake and vibrate. Once in a while, the small glass tube would vibrate out of alignment with the numbers. So to insure you got a more accurate reading of the temperature Daddy would set his thumbnail on the bulb on the small glass tube and gently push the cylinder up a little more. This always guaranteed that it was colder there at the locust tree than any other place on River Ridge. I have even seen it 100° colder than the North Pole. It was like maybe one of those arctic blasts came about 5:30 a.m. every Saturday morning.

In the summer the reverse was true. Pap would gently push the little red alcohol cylinder down. Consequently, it was hotter there under the locust tree than in Key West, Florida.

Why Daddy did this is still a wonder to me. He was fooling no one, but he kept up the game and liked to brag on the temperature. I guess bragging on the temperature was a lot like bragging on who was the first to pick a ripe red tomato or come hog-killing time who could grow the fattest hog, how deep the snow was at your outhouse or who killed the most fish gigging last night. Country boys need things to brag on. Me, I am no different.

In or about 1971, Chuck and me were in the race of our life to grow the first ripe tomato. I was looking pretty good when the flood washed away my tomato plants. This story is just here to show you, the reader, how important that first tomato can be to an Appalachian American!

Fried Green Tomatoes

To be honest here, we ate a lot of tomatoes. We ate railroad boxcar loads of red ones, tons of them big pink ones and truckloads of those we called "German Queens." We did not cull them yellow ones, either. But the yellow ones just did not have enough acid in them to satisfy the needs of a little fat boy setting in the garden on River Ridge with a small blue box of Morton salt.

It is true that we watched the garden right closely for tomatoes with the slightest strip of red. We kind of marked them and stayed away from those. They are the ones that would be needed in a few weeks for tomato biscuits. But, all of those greens ones were fair game and we ate a bunch of those, too. Fried green tomatoes were a Sunday staple!

Now you see, fried green tomatoes on lots of restaurant menus. People living in town eat them. There have even been movies made about them.

Here is what you need:

6 or 8 good-size green tomatoes. You know, ones about the size of a baseball.

Salt: you be the judge on how much you like.

3 cups all-purpose flour

1 teaspoon red pepper

1 teaspoon black pepper

1 cup buttermilk (You can try with sweet milk, but the buttermilk is much better.)

2 eggs; brown ones I hope

1 cup finely ground cornmeal

Some dry bread crumbs if you have them. Old cornbread works well, too.

1 cup good lard

5 or six popcorn kernels

A big cast iron skillet or Dutch oven

A bottle of Texas Pete or Louisiana Sunshine, whichever you like.

Here is what you do:

1. Cut the tomatoes into ½-inch slices and put them in a green glass bowl.

2. Sprinkle some salt on the tomatoes. Not much is needed; you only want them to start to look like they are sweating. Just let them set and soak up the salt until the lard is hot.

3. Put the cast iron skillet on the stove eye and add the lard. When the lard melts, add in the popcorn kernels. When they pop, the lard is hot enough to cook with. You can toss or eat the popcorn!

4. In one bowl, pour the flour, cornmeal, red pepper, black pepper—again some salt if you think you need it.

5. In a second bowl mix the buttermilk and the eggs.

6. When the popcorn pops, dip a slice of tomato in the bowl of buttermilk and eggs and then roll the slice in the flour/cornmeal mixture.

7. Ever so easily, put that slice of green tomato in the hot lard. Slide it around a little before you turn loose of it. This helps to keep the flour/meal from sticking

8. Cook on one side until golden brown (about 2 or 3 minutes), then turn the slice over.

9. Put the fried slices of tomatoes out on a plate with a paper towel to drain. In the old days, we just ate them right off the stove.

Notes for the cook's eyes only:

- I like to let the lard get real hot in the cast iron skillet. If you will do this, few things will ever stick. The pan will get slicker than my head when Colman Hilton shaved it in the fourth grade.
- Food will be less greasy tasting if you cook with hot lard. Hot lard kind of seals the food so grease can't get in.
- Don't let the lard go to smoking. Keep it at the popcorn popping temperature.

Fried Tomato Sandwich

You got it! A fried tomato sandwich, red tomatoes that is, and a little green tomato too. Sounds like a townie thing; but it is real good!

When I was a kid, we ate fried green tomatoes as talked about above, but one day when I was older, I went to dinner at a fancy place in town where they were serving fried tomato sandwiches. I never even read the menu to learn what it was. I thought that it was going to be a fancy tomato sandwich with some of that thick bread with something like basil butter.

I did not even ask what was on it; I just ordered it. Well, when it came I was very pleased and very surprised. It was a thing of true beauty! When the bill came, I thought that I was going to have to start washing dishes and cleaning out bathrooms. I never in my life thought that a tomato sandwich—one with just any bread—could cost so much or taste so good. So I have started to make my own. The ingredients won't cost you more than a dollar, but the taste will be worth all of your time. This I guarantee. After a few times doing this, I have got the recipe down to one I like. Again, it is a little different than the foods I talk about on River Ridge, maybe a little more of town orientation to it. This ort to have a picture made of it!

Here is what you need:

A cast iron skillet

2 shallow serving bowls

1 keen, sharp knife

2 Tablespoons red wine vinegar (Balsamic will work just fine.)

2 Tablespoons red onions chopped as fine as you can cut them

1 teaspoon black pepper

1 or 2 sprigs fresh marjoram and basil, from the pots outside the back door

½ cup good quality olive oil (I have used corn oil, and it worked just fine.)

Some extra corn oil, just to grease the skillet

2 cups blue cheese all crumbled up (Save two or three tablespoons for sprinkling on the sandwiches.)

2 Tablespoons buttermilk

2 large, full, red and firm tomatoes from the garden

1 hard green tomato

A few cups of green lettuce chopped up

At least 8 slices of good thick bacon fried.

If you have a small herb garden out the back door, I suggest a few sprigs of fresh rosemary, thyme and sage—you be the judge of this. If you go with herbs, roughly chop them up.

Salt to taste

A few croutons were served on the original dish I ate. Some of the time I add; some of the time I don't.

Here is what you do:

1. You can blanch the red tomatoes in boiling water for two seconds and pull off the skins. If you wish, you can blanch the green tomato now, too.

2. In a small magic bullet food processor, add the blue cheese and buttermilk. Run the food processor until the mixture is smooth. YOU DO WANT THE MIXTURE TO BE AS THICK AS MOLASSES.) Set mixture aside for a few minutes.

3. In the same small food processor add the vinegar, the onion, black pepper and marjoram and basil. Add in the olive oil, too. (If you have chosen to add the other herbs; go on and put them in the food processor.) Chop the mixture until it turns into a thick salad dressing, again you want the salad dressing to be thick.

4. Cut the green tomato into at least four thick slices. Do not add breading to the green tomato. Now carefully place the slices in a hot cast iron skillet and cook only until tender!

5. If you wish, you can cook the green tomato in a few spoonsful of bacon dripping and not the olive oil.

6. Slice the two red tomatoes and set the bottom halves in a shallow bowl. Here is just a little helpful tip—cut a little piece off the bottom of the red tomato to make it set level.

7. To assemble the sandwich, first add two strips of the bacon, then a few spoonsful of the blue cheese mixture, next a few big spoonsful of the salad dressing, a few pieces of the chopped leaf lettuce and a few blue cheese crumbles. Add the slice of crisp green tomato. Repeat the layers.

8. Don't be afraid to add the last of both the blue cheese mixture and salad dressing to the top of the tomato sandwich. Just let it run down over the sides.

9. When you get to the top, place the ripe tomato up there. Put two long toothpicks in the top to hold the sandwich together and upright. (A broom straw works well.)

Notes for the cook's eyes only:

- There is nothing set in stone. Basil is a wonderful herb for this recipe. Fresh works better than dry. I like the green color it makes in the mixture. I just do not want you to overdo it on the first making.
- Try not to overcook the green tomato. A little crunch is good and the lemon's acid taste of the green tomato adds to the overall taste experience.
- Salt to your taste. Me, I like adding salt at the table.
- If you are a fan of croutons, use very small ones or break the larger ones into smaller ones. You can add a few around the base of the bowl. Put them on top of the lettuce and blue cheese. You don't want them to get too soggy.
- If the layers are getting to be runny, you can add a layer of croutons near the bottom to suck up some the liquid
- If there is any salad dressing and blue cheese dressing or crumbles left, go on and pour it around the bottom of the tomato. Sometimes I even make a few extra crumbles to put around the base of the tomato. Your choice here.

Tomato Gravy

Make it exactly the same way you would make sausage or ham gravy. Here is the difference. Before you even start warming the Dutch oven, take a half gallon of tomato juice and run it through the blender to get rid of the all the lumps of tomato. Substitute the tomato juice for the milk. BUT keep some milk on hand to thin with, kind of like how you'd use the water in the earlier recipe.

Stewed Tomatoes and Dumplings

Just the other day one of my grandchildren asked me to take her to a restaurant that made lots of specialty foods. (People tell me that my little girls have me trained. Well, they are correct, and I just love it.) At this restaurant they had stewed tomatoes, and that made me think back to my childhood and stewed tomatoes and dumplings.

In the summer the one vegetable we had plenty of was tomatoes. Momma was always coming up with different ways to fix tomatoes. One of the best was her fresh stewed tomatoes and dumplings. We almost always had them at supper.

Here is what you need:

A 2-gallon stew pot

About a peck of dead-ripe red tomatoes

1 big hoe cake left over from making biscuits

2 large onions

2 Tablespoons salt

1 teaspoon pepper

2 Tablespoons sugar

6 Big elephant garlic cloves from the garlic patch at the barn gate

Here is what you do:

1. Blanch all the tomatoes in hot water so the skins will come off, then dump them into a dishpan.

2. Peel, remove all the cores and chop into small pieces. You can leave some of the tomatoes just cut in half.

3. Put all the chopped tomatoes back into the stew pot and set them to boiling. As soon as they come to a rolling boil, move the pot to a cooler side of the wood stove. Or you can cut the electric stove down to simmer.

4. Let the tomatoes cook down on low heat until much of the water has been cooked off.

5. Once the tomatoes are thick, you can add the salt and sugar to taste.

6. About one hour before supper, cut the garlic cloves into small pieces and put into the tomatoes.

7. Dice up the onion into good-sized pieces and put into the tomatoes, too.

8. Bring the tomatoes back up to a boil and taste for the seasonings. (Add in more salt or pepper, if needed.)

9. Make up a batch of fresh biscuits and set them to baking.

10. Take the hoe cake (the leftover part after you cut up the biscuit) and mash it back together and cut it into 1-inch pieces and drop them into the boiling tomatoes. You may need 15 little dough squares.

11. Cut the temperature down to a very low boil. All you need to do is cook the dough all the way through. If you get it just

right, the dough will be cooked and dry in the middle.

12. When the dough is done, the tomato dumplings are ready to serve.

Notes for the cook's eyes only:

- I like to cover the top of my tomato dumplings with black pepper. I just might need a small spoonful of sugar, too.
- I would like to suggest that you have a dish of cold cottage cheese and sliced tomatoes. Cold cucumbers and sliced onions covered in vinegar are almost a required condiment.
- Butter for the hot biscuits.
- I like fresh green beans and onions.
- Tall glasses of buttermilk, if you have it. If not, sweet milk will do.
- Fresh cherry cobbler with fresh whipped cream all over the top makes a great dessert.
- Also, if you are into growing fresh herbs, a small handful of oregano, marjoram and thyme are good to add in the very early cooking phase. I like to garnish the dish with a small tree of rosemary.

A "MEAT"ING OF THE MINDS

(AND THE BELLIES)

Charlie Elizabeth's T-bone Steak

Charlie is another eight-year-old grand-daughter who knows what she likes. One day, she and I were alone at home, and I said, "Your grandmother will be coming home soon, so what do you think we should fix her for supper?"

Without even blinking Charlie said, "I think that we should have a steak!"

I answered, "Well you pick it out, and we will fix it." Being a country boy, I try to keep two freezers with a lot of beef. So, Miss Charlie and me start digging through the freezer until we come up with two nice T-bone steaks. I looked at her out of the corner of my eye and said, "Well, do you reckon you and your Granny can eat this for supper?"

Another time when Charlie was helping me, I asked her how much she planned to charge me. She answered, "A steak, mashed potatoes and corn." That is exactly what we had for supper.

We took the steaks into the house and set them on the edge of the sink to thaw out. While the meat was thawing we went to work making up our world-famous "steak marinade."

Steak Marinade

Here is what you need:

½ cup Italian salad dressing

1 teaspoon garlic powder

Onion powder works very well too (or a small onion chopped real fine)

¼ teaspoon cumin

½ teaspoon coriander powder

½ teaspoon lemon pepper

¼ teaspoon salt

½ stick melted butter

2 teaspoons cold coffee

Here is what you do:

1. I mix all the ingredients in a small bowl and transfer them to a large plastic zip-top bag.

2. I place both steaks in the bag and carefully move them around until they are covered with the meat marinade.

3. Then I put the bag in a large bowl, and set it in the refrigerator. I like to keep the steaks refrigerated for about two hours.

4. Personally, I think steak is better when it's grilled outside in the backyard. So, I go build a fire in the wood-burning grill. I like to cook with seasoned maple wood. I clean the racks while the fire is getting hot.

5. Once the fire is a mound of red maple coals, I set the clean racks back on the grill. While they're getting hot, I go get the steaks, put them on the hot racks and close the top.

6. After about four or five minutes, I turn the steaks over. For me, three to four minutes on each side yields a medium-rare steak. Miss Charlie likes her steak a little more done, so I leave hers four or five minutes per side.

While I am cooking, Miss Charlie helps her granny carry out the dishes, salad and vegetables. Once the picnic table is set, we serve the T-bones. But we are not ready to eat yet. Miss Charlie likes the rib-eye side of the T-bone steak, so while the other foods are served, I trim off the rib-eye side and place it on Charlie's plate. I truly do not know if things are going well or not, because she is eating so fast. Me, I like both the top loin and the rib-eye, but I can eat the top loin and get by just fine.

I like to feed Miss Charlie steak. I am on a mission to see her grow tall and have healthy bones. I think beef steak will help on my goal. That, and I like to see her smile!

Notes for the cook's eyes only:

- I admit there are numerous methods for cooking beef steak. Once in a while, we cook steak on one of those electric cookers where the fat runs out. The marinade works well for that cooker, too. Sometimes when no one is looking or it is cold outside, I fry steaks in the big cast iron frying pan like my mother did. This tried and true method works just fine.

- Sometimes I even do not make steak gravy. Neither Charlie nor her grandmother will eat gravy, so I make them au jus sauce. In high-dollar restaurants they call gravy "au jus" sauce. For me and you, we will just call it gravy. But it is so good.

- I think that a baked potato is always welcomed with a crisp lettuce salad. Coleslaw works well, too. Put some red cabbage in it, and the crowd will jump up and down. Strong tea is recommended. Charlie likes milk with hers.

Beef Stew

Beef stew is truly one of the mainstays for about every Appalachian American. When I was little, Mother would put a big roast in a large stew pot and set it on a wood heat stove or on the back of the wood stove. After the meat had cooked down a while, she took out all the bones and added carrots, potatoes, onions, celery, salt and black pepper. Then she refilled the stew pot with water, and let it slowly simmer until suppertime.

The beef stew was thick and creamy. The meat was so tender that each strand of the roast could be separated with a fork. The vegetables were almost gone. They had become part of the stew broth. Life was great when Mother made beef stew. When the leftover stew was allowed to cool, a thick layer of fat formed on the top.

Today I still make beef stew, but I use a little different recipe. My beef stew is much lower in fat than my Mother's. Another thing: I always purchase a local beef each year. This way the cost of hamburger, roast and steak are the same. So when I make good beef stew, I use good quality roast.

When I was a little boy one of my jobs was feeding the small Holstein bottle calves. There were always one or two new ones, baby calves that Daddy had gotten from the Adams Farm. But every year one or two of the calves were sold off as veal calves.

Also, one or two of the calves were kept on the place to grow out for two or more years. They got to be big animals, even bigger pets and were destined to be slaughtered for beef.

Today I hear people talking about grass-fed beef and how good it is. Well, these homegrown beefs were not exactly grass-fed animals, because a month or two before their slaughter they were put in the big hog lot behind the barn. Morning and evening they were fed a quart of cracked corn. This was to start fattening them up for slaughter.

This was a great rural life learning experience. I fed the Holsteins cracked corn. The pigs rooted through the cow droppings for extra corn; the pigs were being fattened too. The chickens ranged freely through the hog lot eating leftover cow dropping and pig manure. The chickens were being fattened, too, for winter and being encouraged to lay more eggs.

When the weather turned cold, long about Thanksgiving Day, animals were slaughtered. The beef was skinned and hung in the big locust tree not far from Grandmother's back window. The pigs went to the scalding box. Today, kids and even some adults would have nightmares if they took part in this fall ritual. To us, it meant a long winter with bellies full of beef stew.

Here is what you need:

6 pounds of roast. Do not cut the meat into cubes, and do not cut any of the fat off the meat.

2 pounds of mushrooms, the smaller, the better

2 large onions, 2 large potatoes, 3 carrots. Just hold onto them; we will cut them up a little later.

2 Tablespoons both salt and garlic

1 Tablespoon black pepper, cayenne pepper, marjoram, thyme, cumin and bay leaves (Use the crumbly kind of bay leaf. I ain't much on looking for the whole bay leaf to pull it out.)

1 Tablespoon of all-purpose flour

Optional ingredients: 1 cup cold coffee and 1 ounce bitter chocolate. I use them, but you may not want to

½ teaspoon both rosemary and ginger

1cup whole milk. Hang onto the milk and use only if you think you need a little extra fluid.

Here is what you do:

1. I like to measure out all of the dry spices into a small bowl and stir them.
2. Put the roast in a large crock pot. Add half of the spices, and let the roast cook six hours on high or until it is falling apart.
3. Take the meat out of the crock pot and set it in the refrigerator overnight. In a second container, collect the liquid. Let it cool and set it in the refrigerator overnight, too. Don't worry if there isn't too much liquid
4. About six hours before you want to serve the beef stew, take both the roast and liquid from the refrigerator and remove the fat layer. Take the potato masher and mash up the meat some to separate the fibers. Put the meat and juices back in a clean crock pot.
5. Turn the crock pot on low.
6. Four hours before serving, stir in the milk and the other

half of the spices and herbs. Let the milk get hot and taste the meat and juices and adjust the spices if need be. It should be a little salty and have a little hot pepper taste. Keep in mind all of the vegetables are yet to be added. Add in the coffee and chocolate.

7. Cut all the vegetables to uniform ½-inch size. About 90 minutes before serving, add the vegetables and give the roast/stew one or two stirs. Turn the crock pot to high.

8. About 30 minutes before serving, add the mushrooms. It might be a good idea to taste and adjust the seasoning and spices.

Notes for the cook's eyes only:

- The goal of the beef stew is to have a dish with very low fat and drier than most beef stews. I want the flavor from the fat. Note, we will remove the fat after the roast has cooked and cooled.

- I hope the meat cooked to pieces and the vegetables cooked and remained tender, still holding their shape and form.

- Also, vegetables and the meat will produce juices.

- Early in the cooking, if there isn't going to be enough juices for you, add a little more milk.

Grilled Pork Loin

When I was a kid we killed hogs every fall. Sometimes we killed hogs for almost the whole community. There could be as many as 15 to 30 hogs dipped in the scald box on a given day. But, only three or four were our own. Possibly, the most cherished cut of meat was the tenderloin. It was more anticipated than even ham biscuits and gravy. A piece of tenderloin sliced about 3/8 of an inch thick, rolled in flour and fried slowly in hot lard and put on a plate with three or four hot butter biscuits covered in tenderloin gravy was about the best meal I ever ate. But I never did have a smoked loin or a grilled pork loin and very few pork chops until I was grown. So you might say that I was ready for a change.

These days I would much rather have a whole pork loin made outside on the grill than pork chops or tenderloin. I even like the loin better than Daddy's neck bones and cabbage. I will tell you about that a little later.

Here is what you need

A 10-pound pork loin

A meat injection needle

A cleaned-off barbeque grill

A small stack of pear or apple wood (I like hickory wood, too.)

2 Tablespoons dry sage

½ cup Italian salad dressing

1 full Tablespoon salt

1 Tablespoon coarsely cracked pepper

1 Tablespoon rosemary

1 Tablespoon garlic salt

A cup of high-quality moonshine that has spent much of its life in an oak keg just waiting for this very day. It is hard to find, but it is still out there.

1 cup of apple juice

Go on and take a little sip from the moonshine cup.

Here is what you do:

1. Take the meat syringe and inject apple juice into the pork loin. This adds flavor and keeps the lion from drying out while cooking. Set the loin on big piece of aluminum foil.

2. Go on and start a fire in your grill. Make a big fire that will generate about three inches of coals. I have an old grill that looks like a barrel that has been cut in half. It has a small smoke stack on it. I start the fire at least two hours before time to eat.

3. On the big piece of aluminum foil I pour out the Italian salad dressing.

4. I sprinkle the salt, garlic salt, pepper, rosemary and sage all over the foil and loin. I use my hands to kind of stir the herbs into the dressing. You can do this without the salt,

but you just cannot do it without the pepper.

5. Place the pork loin on the aluminum foil and slowly turn the loin over and over until it is uniformly coated with herbs and salad dressing. Just leave the loin wrapped up in the foil until the grill and coals are the proper temperature.

6. I like to put the pork loin on the upper grill farthest from the coals when the temperature comes down to 200^0.

7. I then paint the remainder of the herbs and dressing on the pork loin.

8. About every 15 minutes I paint the loin with moonshine that has a nice oak flavor from the keg. The alcohol burns off as the meat cooks. The goal is to infuse that wonderful moonshine flavor into the meat. Be careful. The grill will fire up when you spread on the shine!

9. I do not have a meat thermometer, though I do think that I am getting one for Christmas this year. It is something that I would like to have. I cook the pork loin until the pink color of the meat is gone. I remove the meat from the grill and let it rest on a clean plastic cutting board for 5 to 10 minutes, then slice it into 3/8 inch slices if there are a lot coming to eat. If not so many are coming, I cut the meat a full ½ inch or a little more.

10. I do this, but you may be one of the lucky people with a meat thermometer, so you probably know when the meat reaches an internal temperature of 145^0 it is done. Be real careful to not overcook it.

Notes for the cook's eyes only:

- I like grilled red onions with pork loin.

- I like to fry hard red and yellow apples in butter and put them on one end of the serving plate with the onions on the other. I place the pork loin all around the apple and onions and let the dish set for just minute so the apple, onion and pork juices can mix some.
- I like the meal with a big garden salad with fresh tomatoes.
- How about roasted rutabaga, turnips, carrots, winter squash and potatoes with lots of garlic, butter and rosemary?
- I also like a tall glass of icy cold tomato juice.
- I think a large cabbage head cut into about eight wedges and slowly boiled until tender then painted with butter and covered with fresh rosemary, parsley and thyme is awful good.

Another Pork Loin Recipe

I do not use a smoker. Call me old-fashioned, but I like to cook this pork loin recipe on an old charcoal grill, one that looks like a half of a barrel. Before we go on much further, I need to let you in on something. Some say that I am tighter than "Dick's Hat Band." I don't think of me in that light at all. I like to think of me as, well, say "thrifty."

At one time, I did not have a good grill. One morning I am headed out to work and my neighbor up the road has dragged out an old half-barrel grill to the road for trash. All day I thought about his old grill, and it did not look all that worn out to me. So late that night, I walked up the road and looked the grill over. Under the cloak of darkness and the quiet of night, I take aholt of the grill and slowly start rolling it down the road to my house. I had not gone more than thirty feet when one of the wheels fell off. It made a lot of noise, but not more than ten houses turned on their lights to check out the clatter. Within the next thirty feet, the other wheel fell off and made a big clanking noise. This time, every light on the street came on, and everyone watched me drag the grill from the trash of one house to my home.

I now have a real good old grill that cooks like a brand new one. It smells great when smoke is rising from its tall stack. You know, me and that old grill have lot in common. We both are old, we both have some rust on us, and we both are round around the middle.

This is not a smoker grill. It is just your regular old charcoal grill. I use wood for cooking. In the small woodshed I keep a stack of white oak, hard maple and cherry (not wild cherry but wax cherry wood from an old cherry orchard).

When I cook pork loin, I like to use maple wood. About five hours before I want to serve the loin, I build a big fire in my grill. I try to add in almost all the wood that I will be using to cook with, so I pile the grill full of seasoned maple blocks from the wood house. Most of the blocks are cut into six- or eight-inch pieces. I let the blocks burn until a thick layer of red coals form in the bottom of the grill. After the wood is burning very hot I close the top of the grill and open up the side air vent. I want the wood to still burn, but I like for it to turn into a hard wood charcoal.

I keep a close eye on the grill's thermometer. When the grill is holding a temperature of 250^0. I maintain this temperature. I put the pork loin on the grill and add a little salt and pepper to it. I pour or brush one half of the dressing gently over the meat and cook it slowly. Before I turn the meat over, I very, very carefully stick my fingers in a quart of moonshine and sprinkle it over the loin until the charcoal flames up. This creates a wonderful dark bark on the meat.

After the pork loin has been on the grill for about 45 minutes, I turn it over and season the other side with the remaining dressing and salt and pepper. Again, I sprinkle the moonshine over the meat, and again the flames try to kiss it. Once the inside temperature of the pork loin has reached 145^0, I take it off the grill. I want the pork fully cooked, but not overcooked. Once the pink has disappeared it is done. I let the loin rest on the cutting board for twenty minutes before slicing.

Here is what you need:

One or two full pork loins, washed and allowed to come to room temperature.

A grill filled with hard maple charcoal burning at a temperature of 250°.

Marmalade, soy sauces and spices—see below.

Here is what you do:

1. Take a small paint brush and wipe the grill with corn oil. This may help keep the meat from sticking.
2. Place the meat on the grill and close the lid.
3. In a 2-quart saucepan, dump three 12-ounce jars of peach marmalade, 3 ounces of soy sauce, possibly a sprinkle of red pepper— about ¼ teaspoon.
4. Warm the sauce very slowly and stir it constantly.
5. The second the sauce looks like it is going to boil, get it off the stove.
6. Pour 1/3 of the sauce into a measuring cup. This will be used as a sauce when serving the pork loin.
7. Go to the grill and carefully start spooning the sauce on the pork loin.
8. Cook for 45 minutes. Just before turning loins over, evenly cover the meat with moonshine. Be careful of the flames.
9. Turn the loins over and repeat the process of adding the sauce and moonshine.

10. When the meat is up to 145^0 take it off the grill, and let it stand for 20 minutes.
11. Then slice the pork loin into 3/8 inch slices.
12. Serve with a teaspoon of the peach/soy sauce.

Notes for the cook's eyes only!

- If you have a double boiler, it would be nice for making the sauce.
- I do not marinate the pork loin using this recipe.
- If you wish, you can inject a small amount of moonshine into the pork loin. This does add a lot of flavor.
- Salt and pepper to your taste.
- Again, I like it cooked this way with red onions.

Fresh-Killed Pork Backbones

When I was a kid, we butchered lots of hogs. But we almost never ate pork chops. Instead, we ate tenderloin, and it was not just good—it was great! As a result, we ate a lot of backbones, too. Backbones are always good, but there is an art to cooking them. If you are doing the hog-killing, make sure that you leave a little extra tenderloin on the backbones. The meatier they are, the better. I caution you not to run yourself short on tenderloin.

Here is what you need.

About 4 pounds of right meaty backbones. Take a few seconds to wipe them down real good. Make sure you get all the bone shards off the meat.

4 ounces King's corn syrup right out of the big metal can. Honey will do in a pinch. Once in awhile Daddy would use maple syrup to add a little variety to our diet.

1 cup ketchup

½ cup apple cider

2 fresh cloves garlic, pulled from the patch by the gate leading to the barn and chopped fine.

2 Tablespoons tangy mustard

1 teaspoon hot cayenne pepper

1 teaspoon salt and 1 teaspoon black pepper

1 Tablespoon melted lard

Combine all of the ingredients and set the mixture on the back of the stove to warm.

Here is what you do:

1. Pre-heat the oven to 375^{0}.

2. In a big cast iron pot, boil the backbones for 30 minutes.

3. Take the backbones out of the water to drain and cool. (You can save the water for backbone gravy if you want to.) An awful lot of people keep this water for gravy.

4. In a mixing bowl measure out the syrup, ketchup, apple cider, mustard, garlic, cayenne pepper, black pepper and salt. It is important to set the bowl in a very warm place so the syrup can soften and mix well with the other spices.

5. In a cast iron Dutch oven, spread a very thin layer of lard all over the bottom and sides, and then place the backbones one layer thick, if possible.

6. Pour the warm sauce over the backbones. Make sure that each piece is coated with sauce.

7. Bake for 20 to 25 minutes. Keep in mind the backbones have already boiled some and are almost cooked.

8. Cook until the meat is starting to separate from the bone and the sauce is bubbling good.

9. Remove from the oven and stir around in the thick, sticky sauce and pour the backbones into a large serving bowl. Daddy always used one of the ones that looked like a big ear

of corn. You do not want to lose any of the juices. (If the sticky juice gets on the floor, you might have to pull up a piece of tile to remove it. Get it on your shoe and step on the concrete and you will pull the sole off-n your shoe for sure! Makes you wonder what is going on down in your stomach, don't it?)

10. Serve hot right out of the oven.

Notes for the cook's eyes only:

- Choose backbones with a lot of tenderloin still on them.
- Cook backbones real slow.
- Serve with a large bowl of pinto beans.
- Chow-chow for the beans.
- Cornbread for the smallish dish beside your big dish, and butter, of course.
- A dish of turnip greens or mustard greens.
- Sweet tea and buttermilk if you have it. The tangy taste of the buttermilk will help to cut the thick sweet taste.
- The last of this season's tomatoes sliced up right thick.
- Most important, handfuls of napkins, because you are going to need them!
- Ample amounts of coleslaw.

Chasing a Buck Deer Across New River

The year is 1968, Chuck Shorter and me are floating down river. We are just below the Old Bus and right about the barrel on the rock bar. The water is flat and blue as indigo. The only thing that breaks the blue color is the reflection of the fall colors of the trees on shore, and red and orange leaves in the tranquil water. It is truly one of those days only true Appalachian Americans can say they have seen. A few non-Appalachian people may think they have seen days like this, but I can bet oh so very few have ever been caught in a river like this.

The old wooden john boat is drifting downriver at the speed of New River's current. My old 2-horsepower Elgin air-cooled motor is setting full of gas not running. It is ready, though, when we need it to make the turn back up the river. The view of the coming rock bar, the closeness of the big island and little island, and the view between the islands of the big farm and green is resting peacefully on my mind.

In less than a second the world can change. Out of the corner of my eye, a nice-sized buck deer comes running off the bank near Grissom's Cabin and jumps in the water close to the barrel by the rock bar. The deer was about half running and about half swimming. (Years earlier, Mr. Grissom had carried a metal barrel out to the rock bar. There he stood it up and filled it with rocks. You could now look at the barrel and tell the level of the river water.)

“Catch him,” screamed Chuck. That mighty 2-horsepower Elgin roared to life. We were now in hot pursuit of that buck deer. More realistically, I was just hoping to get close. The motor was just one shade faster than polling the boat. Chuck reaches down into the boat and picks up the boat chain and ties a knot in the chain.

“You ain’t going to pitch that over his head are you?” I said. I am thinking, “You drag that thing into this boat, he will kill us with his feet.” I did not care. I was in on this race, and it was fun!

“Faster,” hollers Chuck.

I have the Elgin wound up tighter than the big spring in a Swiss watch. The power and strength of that Elgin were just great enough to pull us up close to the deer. Then all of sudden the buck seemed to grab another gear, and he was soon outpacing us. No, we did not catch the deer, but we thought about it.

It is so funny how the facts of a story can change over the years. Later when I told the story, I told people that the deer was far downriver a good ways, and my little motor carried us downriver so fast that we ran past the massive big, big buck deer. The john boat was going so fast that I just could not slow it down. If I could have stopped we would have been eating “Chicken Fried Deer Steak” for a week. “I can just smell them steaks frying now. The smell fills the whole house,” says old me.

Chicken Fried Deer Steak

Here is what you need:

4 or 5 pounds of round steaks with the bone removed

A large cast iron Dutch oven

A cup or more of lard

A cup or two of flour

2 eggs beaten and 1 cup of milk mixed in a bowl

2 Tablespoons salt

2 Tablespoons black pepper

1 teaspoon garlic

1 teaspoon cumin

A dash or two of any other herbs you like

The old wooden chopping board

The meat hammer

Here is what you do:

1. Wash off the cutting board and meat hammer.
2. Put the Dutch oven on the stove to get hot with a tablespoon of lard.
3. Hammer each steak for a while. Hammer them down until they are about 3/8 of an inch or less in thickness. Being thin don't hurt a chicken-fried steak. The goal is make them real tender.

4. When the lard is hot, dip one steak in the egg and milk, then roll it in the flour. Carefully, place it in the hot lard.

5. Do this again until all the steaks are cooked. Add more lard as needed.

6. Scrape all the brown cooked flour from the bottom of the Dutch oven. You can dump the remainder of the flour into the Dutch oven for making gravy, if you want to.

Notes for the cook's eyes only:

- I put the egg and milk wash in the hog feed bucket. I don't think that it would make good gravy.
- Salt and pepper to taste.
- Chicken-Fried Steak is real good with boilt potatoes and hot butter biscuits

Baked Ham that Ain't No Ham at All

About once every two months I have to make myself a Spam sandwich. I know that I should not be telling people that I eat much Spam, but I do and I like the stuff. I eat it lots of ways. I like to cut up a thick slice and fry it until it is brown around the edges and put it on two slices of crispy toasted white bread with tomatoes, lots of lettuce leaves, salt, pepper and mayonnaise. I love to carry Spam with me when I go hunting. It is easy and convenient to cut little pieces up and put them on saltine crackers. I think those small cans were made just for me. Yes, I can eat a whole small can—cold right out of the can. Thank goodness for Spam.

Possibly the absolute best way to eat Spam is baked like a small ham. When I was a kid, Mother baked a lot of Spam when we had company come over. This was not that often.

I saw a fellow in the Piggly Wiggly the other day. He is a person I have known all of my life, but somebody I never ever had one thing in common with. Until this very day. When I picked up three cans of Spam and put them in my grocery buggy, I said to myself, "The weatherman was calling for snow, and I do not want to be out of spam." Then I saw this man looking at me. I just knew he was going to say something about me eating Spam, him being a town-type person and all.

"I see you picked up a few cans of Spam," said the nice fellow.

"Me, too. I eat Spam about once a week. You know, I have heard it isn't the best thing in the world for me to eat, but I am just like my father. He ate Spam once or twice a week to the day he died. He got hooked on the stuff during World War II."

When you get right down to it, I think that it is funny how alike people are.

Momma would make toasted Spam sandwiches when I was sleigh-riding. I ate them with hot soup. Back in 1960, there was nothing better.

We ate Spam and eggs for breakfast. Cold Spam sandwiches for lunch with slices of red tomato and lettuce. Spam chunks in soups. The list of Spam delicacies goes on. Never know, there might be some Hawaiian crossed in me. Never Know!

When I was working for 4-H I took a group of young people to a volunteer's house to make bird houses. This was a real nice volunteer lady in a wonderful neighborhood. Just before lunch time, she just up and vanished. In few minutes she came back with a whole tray of sandwiches for lunch. There was your Spam and mayonnaise on white bread, spam and tomato on toast, even a few Spam sandwiches with cheese. Me, I jumped right in and ate a great Spam on toast sandwich. The others would not eat anything. I think that whole generation has just missed out on the grandeur of Spam.

Here is what you need:

4 cans of Spam (You need that much for an average family like mine.)

A small spice can of whole cloves

A can of pineapple rings (Crushed will do if you are in a rush.)

A cast iron Dutch oven or any oven pan

Here is what you do:

1. Remove the Spam from the cans.
2. Place all four little "hams" on a baking pan or cast iron pan. They can be touching if you wish.
3. Put maybe 8 or 10 whole cloves in each piece.
4. Cover with pineapple rings (You just might need a few toothpicks to hold the pineapple rings in place.)
5. Put the pan in the oven at 350^0 until the Spam is hot all the way through and the pineapple rings are starting to brown.

Notes for the cook's eyes only:

- I like my Spam served just like small canned ham. You know, a few hot biscuits, sweet milk, and fried potatoes with onions. Spam is good with brown beans, too.
- Try Spam with fried green tomatoes.
- A dish of sweet potatoes is good, too.
- You want something else to reduce the taste of the fatty texture of the Spam.

Apple and Sausage Pie

Two things happened just recently that brought this recipe back to mind. Not too long ago I was visiting my brother Melvin, and he cooked a dish similar to this. It was just wonderful! A few days back Miss Gail purchased a large glass pie dish, and I just started to think back. When I was little, every once in a while both Mamma and Grandmother would make sausage apple pies. They were as good as anything on the supper table. Also, I now realize the Sausage and Apple Pie was just another way the ladies on the River Ridge dreamed up to insure that no food was wasted. Read on and you will see what I am talking about. In Mother's time she made a fresh pie crust; today I just purchase one from Kroger.

Here is what you need:

Go on and turn the oven on to 375^0.

1 pound medium-seasoned sausage. Crumble up the sausage and cook it. Set it in a colander to drain out.

2 cups hard apples cut into thin slices

2 cups grated cheese—Swiss or Monterey Jack I think are the best for this job.

¾ cup heavy fresh cream, the thicker the better.

2 spoonsful fresh yellow butter set on the stove to melt

4 eggs

2 Tablespoons all-purpose flour

1 teaspoon salt

1 teaspoon black pepper

¼ teaspoon sage

Here is what you do:

1. Put the pie shell in a baking dish and layer the sausage and apple onto it.

2. Put the salt, flour, sage and pepper in a mixing bowl and stir it around. Then add the cream, cheese and eggs and mix well.

3. Now pour the mixture over the sausage and apples and let it stand on the counter for a minute or two to let the liquid soak down into the pie.

4. Bake the pie for 45 minutes. You need to make sure the eggs are cooked.

5. Take the pie out of the oven and let it again stand on the counter for five minutes.

Notes for the cook's eyes only:

- Me, I like the pie for supper with shell beans, strong tea and sweet potatoes.
- If you do this in the summer and fall, fresh tomatoes are good.
- Note: if you use canned sausage, often the sausage is packed in a quart jar so you may need to adjust the recipe some.

Grilling an Old Sheep

The year was 1972, and the month was February. My winter had been spent living in my very own cinderblock house on the river just above the two islands. Life was great, the winter had not been too cold. But there was an icy wind off the river cold enough to cut your ears off. Somehow I had kept up a fire in the fireplace. For no reason at all the weather changed. A very warm spell occurred in late February, and with it the emergence of an old, old ewe. Yes, this old ewe had a Grover Cleveland campaign button on.

This old animal had fared very well through the winter, but the owner of the animal said she did not have a lamb this year so he was going send her over to the livestock market in Christiansburg. "She is so old that it will cost more in gas to carry her to the stockyard than she will sell for." Just out of the blue, me along with the two or three friends with me said in unison, "We will take the ewe and barbeque her."

As we load her into my old pickup, my friends said they'd help out with this. It was going to be fun. We would invite everybody to the barbeque. I was truly into it, too.

So we started make a list of the things that we needed to do. Where to cook the sheep? How to cook it? How to tell people? What to cook the animal on? Sauce? Firewood? Beer? And more beer? All of a sudden we realized we had a lot to do.

First things first. The old ewe was butchered and hung high in a tree near the river. Later the carcass was transferred to my refrigerator for storage. On the bank outside the cabin, Chuck, Melvin, Wimpy and maybe David Price and others built a makeshift barbeque grill out of cinderblocks. A quick trip was made to the Hoot Owl Woods in search of a piece of expanded metal to make the grill top. This was done when it was real quiet, because this property belonged to Virginia Tech and they just might not have loaned us the piece of metal if they had known what it was for.

We scoured the country for every piece of old, hard wood stump, old oak lumber or hickory limb that could be carried to the cabin. We told everyone we crossed that they were invited to the cabin on Saturday night for a LAMB barbecue. Notice how the sheep changed from an old, tough mutton to a tender young lamb.

Come Saturday, the February air temperature was more like late spring than late winter. People had been locked under covers for a long time, and I think they must have wanted out, too. Everyone who had been asked came with a covered dish from off the stove. They also brought friends with them. It turned out to be a great break from the winter's cold wind. In a few days the temperature would grow cold and them cutting winds blow up river once again. Everybody was talking about grilled lamb! I think more than fifty people came out.

Something else started that February day. We started grilling every slow animal that passed us by. Over the next three or four years we cooked deer, chickens, sheep and an occasional pig. I think we stopped only because we ran out of wood. Others had other thoughts. I announced one day that I was getting married. One response was, "Well, there goes them River Barbeques."

Unbeknownst to me, my cousin was right. Come that fall I found myself enrolled in the University of Rhode Island, and there was a salty ocean out my door rather than the sweet water of New River. No, I never did have another barbeque on the river bank.

A little note for the reader. After awhile my brother, Melvin, made us a permanent stone grill. It was complete with a native stone exterior and a firebrick lining. It was a great grill. Possibly its most interesting feature was the fact that we placed the grill about 10 feet from the outdoor toilet. The toilet was an old telephone booth, complete with the glass doors. Handy for the cook, but not so for the person wanting to use the toilet. Ladies did a lot of leg-crossing until dark.

Here is what you need:

One cleaned and dressed sheep/ewe/lamb or about 60 pounds of lamb meat. I cut the carcass into four pieces

A big stack of clean fire wood—no painted boards and no treated lumber!

About a gallon of barbeque sauce

Here is what you do:

1. Kill and process the sheep at least two days before you want to cook.
2. Set up the cooking pit. This is very important, because you want the meat to cook real slowly. I like to have the meat at least 30 inches above the heat. I think—just me here thinking—the slower tough meat cooks the more tender it is.
3. I start a small fire a few feet from the cook pit. Here I burn

large pieces of wood into something resembling charcoal. These pieces I evenly put in the barbeque pit. Again, I do not want a big fire. Let the meat cook for five or six hours if that is what it takes.

4. About every 20 minutes I splash on the barbeque sauce.

5. Cook to an internal temperature of about 145^0. In the old days we cooked the meat until it was just a very light pink in the middle. (When I was a youth, occasionally the Blue Ribbon Beer may have affected my ability to see all the colors of the rainbow.) You do whatever you want to.

The Barbeque Sauce

Here is what you need:

A two-gallon stew pot

2 maybe 4 hot pads for lifting the pot. No need to scald to death at a barbeque

3 quarts vinegar

2 quarts ketchup

1 pound salt

4 ounces black pepper

2 ounces red pepper

3 pounds dark brown sugar

Here is what you do:

1. Mix the ingredients with a big wooden spoon.

2. Set the sauce on the stove using a very low heat setting.

3. DON'T take your eyes off the sauce for not even a second because when it gets hot it is going to come out of the two-gallon pot!

Notes for the cook's eyes only:

- The smell of the sauce has the ability to clean out your sinuses, so keep your handkerchief close! It is potent stuff!
- Once the sauce is hot. Set it off the stove and taste it. Add more of anything you wish. You can play with ingredients in the sauce. I like mine to be a might salty, a bit spicy hot (but not too) and the vinegar flavor is important as well. You can use store-bought if you wish.
- When you're finished and the sauce is cool, put some in a quart jar for dipping sauce when eating. The remainder will be used when cooking.
- Refrigerate both sauces.
- I like to have a light tangy, spicy bark on the goat or sheep.
- Any picnic foods are great! Scalloped potatoes, green beans, fried okra, hot breads. . . I mean anything on the stove
- I set the goat on a big metal tray with a sharp knife, and the guests get what they want.
- I did cook a goat or two when I lived in West Tennessee using this same exact method and sauce recipe. I was real careful not to do this too often. No sir, people kind of get hooked on coming to your house for fine barbeque. It is the sauce, I think. It is good. I have used it on chicken, pork, sheep and goat.

Visitors!

Well, once upon a time I had houseguests who not only were town people, they were Muslim and could not eat my pork or any of my freezers of beef.

After awhile, my visitors got tired of smelling my food and wanted meat to eat. "Uncle Charles, (that is me) we need meat. Is there a place around here where we could buy a lamb?" they asked me.

"Well, no, there ain't a lamb in the country. What few there were have already gone to market. Those few that were left the damned old coyotes ate. I can get you goat, but you have got to go and kill it."

Since about the eighth grade Chuck Shorter has always been my go-to man. So we go to Chuck for a goat.

I ask the family to have a meeting with their children. They have never seen an animal slaughtered. Another thing, there is a very special way the animal must be slaughtered for the meat to be kosher. I want the children and the others to have the opportunity to stay home, because this is not a pretty picture for town people or young. Basically, the animal is taken to the ground and a very short prayer is said thanking "Allah" for this animal and the meat. Then the animal's throat is cut and the animal's allowed to bleed out. Not very pretty, but this is the way it is done.

We drive to Chuck's farm, and there is a field full of goats. Now, when I say we drove to the farm that is what I mean. All crowded in a truck are me, my friend and four kids. Good fat goats are everywhere. "Which goat do we get?"

"You go talk with Chuck, and he will get you the best goat here."

Chuck finds the best young and tender buck goat and turns the animal over to my friend. As the animal's throat is cut the kids look away. Me too! But then they come right back and watch blood pumped from the animal's body. We skin the goat and cut it up. We make six big pieces of meat and head for home.

When we get home, everyone calls the animal a lamb. I don't think that they had ever eaten a goat. When I was in West Tennessee we had a goat for every Fourth of July Celebration. Good tender meat.

Well, I wrap the meat and put it in the deep freezer. They all wanted to know exactly what it was. I think that they did not want to take a chance on pulling out an unkosher piece of meat. No one said this, but I know what they were thinking.

That night we had goat (I mean lamb shoulder) for supper. And it was great! If you ever have the chance to eat goat fixed up right you ort to do it.

Goat Shoulder

I guess this is made in the style of Tom's Creek. We sure did not have this on River Ridge!

Here is what you need:

One real big cast iron Dutch oven. Not one with legs on it.

½ cup olive oil—save enough to coat the bottom of the cast iron Dutch oven

1 Tablespoon salt (The kind in the blue box is fine.)

1 Tablespoon coarse ground black pepper

1 teaspoon curry powder

10 fresh large garlic cloves

1 teaspoon Herbs of Provence (I do like Herbs of Provence because of the lavender in the mixture of herbs. It smells very good cooking.)

1 goat shoulder, 10 to 15 pounds. A whole shoulder is used.

5 stalks celery

4 turnips

4 large onions,

4 potatoes

4 carrots

A small handful of parsley, oregano, basil; a very small handful of rosemary; a small piece or two of mint

A very large green glass bowl

Here is what you do.

1. Pour the half-cup of olive oil (minus that little bit) into the green glass bowl.

2. Wash and peel the potatoes, carrots, onions, and turnips. The celery doesn't need to be peeled. Cut all the vegetables into cubes about ½-inch or less. Now dump them into the green bowl, too. Stir with a fork.

3. All of the fresh herbs are coarsely chopped and added to the bowl. Stir with a fork.

4. Measure out all the dry herbs into a ramekin and lightly mix. Hold onto these herbs until you add the goat shoulder.

5. Turn the oven on to 400^0. Pour off a little of the olive oil from the vegetables into the cast iron Dutch oven. That is if you forgot to save back a little. Go on and put the Dutch oven in the real oven to warm up. It does not need to get all the way to 400^0 —just good and warm.

6. Once the pan is good and warm, take it out of the oven and slowly add all vegetables. With a fork smooth them out across the pan.

7. Now carefully lay the goat shoulder on top of the vegetables. Sprinkle half of the dry herbs on top of the goat shoulder, then turn it over and sprinkle the other half on the meat.

8. Put the top back on the pan and cook until the meat is falling off the bone.

9. Take it out of the oven and let it set for or a few minutes.

Notes for the cook's eyes only:

- Just hang on; this is going to work out!
- I place the whole shoulder on a large meat plate.
- Goat meat is very light in flavor, but cooked this way it is kind of stringy, so you just have to pull off what you want.
- Scoop out all of the vegetables and put them in a serving bowl.
- We had a very thin loaf of white bread with olive oil painted on the top—served hot right out of the oven.
- A green tossed salad with a balsamic salad dressing and oil.
- A soup made from potato, carrots, onions and basil.
- Fresh oranges cut into quarters.
- Very sweet tea—hot tea.
- A salty thick tomato and roasted pepper dish.
- Vanilla ice cream.
- Tall glasses of ice water.

Opossums

Here is a story that I thought that I would never write or never be encouraged to write. I do not care where I am signing copies of New River: bonnets, apple butter and moonshine someone will ask me about catching, cooking and or eating a possum. "Have you ever eaten one of them?" Well, here goes. Possum is kind of a fall food. For me, most possums are caught when a fellow goes "Coon Hunting." Possum is about as wild a food as there is!

The truth is I have only eaten possum once or twice in my life that I am aware of. This took place in and around the time Aunt Tootie cooked the muskrat for Arnold Lytton. That ort to be a story on its own!

Spivey Lyles Westerman lived in the community of Walton. He and Daddy worked together at the Radford Army Ammunition Plant. They kind of hung around a lot there for a while. I think that Mr. Spivey Westerman was more of a bootlegger and moonshiner than a close family friend. Daddy and he just might have run a little licker together once upon a time.

Well, back to the possum. It all happened right quick. Kind of like when Arnold handed me leg of some wild meat—something about the size of squirrel leg—and said "Eat it. It is good!" It turned out to be muskrat. Arnold was right. Muskrat wasn't bad.

The possum leg was just picked up from Mr. Westerman's kitchen table and handed to me. No words were said at all. I just took the hind leg of what I thought was either a wild rabbit or squirrel. I quietly ate the hind leg; it was good. But then again anything rolled in flour and fried right crispy can't help but be good. After a while, I was asked, "What was that you just ate?"

I answered, "I think it is either a rabbit or a squirrel."

"No boy, she was a big sow possum. My young blue tick treed that possum a few weeks ago."

I just got right green around the gills and smiled and said it tasted a lot like a squirrel and was ok. Truly, my first possum was good. I thought it was better than eating horse meat or an old coon dog.

My second try was more like what I had expected. To be honest here, I can't remember who the fellow was. The locals in the community of "Big Gate," West Virginia, just called the homeowner "Founder." My second possum-eating all kind of happened by accident. We had taken an old chain saw over to Founder's house to see if he could get the thing running. He was the local small engine mechanic. We were welcomed into the old house, chain saw and all. The old saw was set right up on the kitchen table to be repaired. My companion said, "If we have come at a bad time, we can come back later."

"No, supper ain't ready yet anyways. I will look at your chain saw," answered Founder. The house was somewhat dirty, and Founder wasn't the neatest fellow I had ever seen either. So the chain saw setting on the kitchen table did not look too much out of place.

In a few minutes we were asked to set down and a have glass of sweet tea. Tea turned into a bite of supper. "Set and eat while I tinker with this chain saw."

I did not want to do this, but the man I was with just set down. Again, I did not want to do this, but Founder had done moved the chain saw over to the side of the kitchen table to make more room. Me, I just set down, too. Mrs. Founder quickly swiped her apron across the table where the chain saw was setting. I never did get Mrs. Founder's name. Somewhere during the meal I heard the name Gorman said. So I think Founder's name was Founder Gorman, but you cannot prove this by me. But Mrs. Founder? Well I do not know. Life in the mountains is still very simple and private. What you don't need to know you ain't told!

The possum wasn't fried, but more baked. The meat was falling off the bone down into the bottom of the cast iron pan. I thought that it was a raccoon that I was being served. I had had coon lots of times before and found it to be somewhat greasy and right gamey on its own. It was all right, but I did not like it. We were served fresh small potatoes from the cellar, sweet tea and hot biscuits and baked or roasted or cooked somehow wild meat.

The potatoes and peas were good, and the tea hit the spot. I dipped apple butter from a quart jar for my biscuits. They were good, too. "Do you want some more meat?" Mrs. Founder asked me.

"No, Mrs. Gorman, I wasn't very hungry when we came over, so I think I will pass. Besides the family has supper ready."

This meat was very greasy and kind of bland tasting. From the first bite, I knew it wasn't squirrel or rabbit. I kind of thought that it might be a possum, so I ate as little as possible. I knew that it was cooked done and OK to eat, because it was cooked to the point it was falling off the bone. It might have helped if the meat had been dipped up out of the grease and let drain. It was so greasy that the meat left a thick film in my mouth, and I could taste it long after I left the Founders' home.

The truth be known, it wasn't bad at all. I have eaten beef and pork that wasn't any better. It was sure better than the heart worm medicine that I ate down at my sister Oleta's house. Now that was almost heart-stopping. I think that it is the thought of eating possum that is so bad. On River Ridge I wasn't exposed to meats like possum or horse or dog or goat. So I just grew up knowing I did like the pork and beef. Same thing with goat kidney. Recently, I was served goat kidney and ate it not knowing what it was. It was OK, but once I was told about the name of the meat I did not ask for any more. As a child I was told that kidney was OK as long as all the pee was boilt out of it.

Me, I'd much rather have a big hamburger or baked ham

So how do I answer the question, how do I fix possum?

I never let on that I have never cooked a possum! But I have had enough old-timers tell me how that I think this answer is about true.

First: It is a proven practice to catch up your possum and cage him for a few weeks. Never, ever, cook a fresh-killed possum. The unwritten rule is the animal must be caged for a minimum of two weeks! The longer he is cage-fed the better. As for me, six months would not hurt him one bit; never know, it might do him some good. Also, be real careful of the possum's teeth. The rascal may have two or three sets of razor-sharp, needle-like teeth, and he will not hesitate to bite you with all of them.

So, you catch up your possum and put him in one of your old rabbit hutches and then start feeding him full of clean green grass and clover every day and lots of fresh clean water. Please keep an eye out for those teeth! After a few days, the possum will figure what is fixing to take place and just might not like the idea of what is going on.

The possum needs to be thinned down a little, so you know his body is cleaning out all the old things he has eaten in the past. So you keep him on a grass and water diet for week or so. Then you can give him all the table scraps you want. Some people like to give him lots of fresh cabbage leaves. Others are insistent upon giving him cracked corn. This is supposed to make the possum grow a layer of new, clean fat.

My overriding question to people always was, "If a possum needs so much cleaning out and thinning down and then it be re-fattened, why do we even want to eat him?"

Next: After the caging phase has been accomplished, it is time to butcher the possum. In doing so, be extra careful and don't let the hair touch the meat. Why, I don't know, that is just what the old-timers said. So, go on and butcher him and soak the meat in cold saltwater over night.

Here is what you need, I think:

In a large cast iron frying pan, add two cups of lard and set it on the stove to get hot.

In a large bowl add two cups of white flour

1 Tablespoon black pepper

½ Tablespoon salt

½ teaspoon garlic powder

2 cups cold milk

Here is what you do, I am supposing:

1. You are free to add in any of your family spices for fried possum now. Also, if you have any fresh herbs in flower pots out back, this would be a good time to chop up a handful. Just put them in the flour.

2. I would suggest that you dry off the meat and set it aside in another bowl.

3. Put three or four popcorn kernels in the lard. When they pop it is time to put the possum in the frying pan. Possum is right greasy to start with, and you don't want any more extra grease cooked into the meat.

4. Pour 2 cups of milk (some use cream) into a small bowl.

5. When the popcorn pops, dip a piece of possum in the milk, then roll it a time or two in the seasoned flour and slowly place it in the hot lard. BE REAL CAREFUL NOT TO GET BURNED.

6. Turn it over once or twice. When the possum turns golden brown all over, it is done.

7. Starting to sound a lot like frying chicken, ain't it? But, truly it ain't.

8. Have the table set and set all the food on your plates when the possum comes out of the lard! I think possum must be eaten hot before the grease starts to get cold! This is real important!

Notes for the cook's eyes only:

- Me, I really don't think you ort to cook this!
- I think that a tall glass of sweet milk is imperative.

- Fall greens with a lot of onion, vinegar, salt and pepper.
- Hot biscuits or cornbread with thick yellow cow butter.
- Fresh potatoes fried with a few turnips are always welcome at mealtime.
- Hot, fresh-perked coffee might be a good idea to help cut the fat stuck to the roof of your mouth.
- NO gravy, please! I think possum would make gravy, but I don't think it would be good.
- Again, do not have side dishes setting in serving bowls on the table. Have them already on your plate when the possum comes out of the pan!

Bon appetit!

FIRST, YOU CATCH THE CHICKEN,

THEN . . .

COLONEL SANDERS MOVE OVER!

Chicken Pot Pie

When I was a youngster, I must have eaten chicken pot pie about every way there was. Most of the time, we ate it in the spring and late fall. In the spring, when new pullets were starting to lay, the old chickens that did not lay eggs anymore found their way to the kitchen. Also chicken pot pie was on the menu again in the late fall, when another round of chickens stopped laying eggs. We did not want to feed them through the winter, so their heads were chopped off, and the old hens were eaten. Often these chickens were as old as Methuselah and very tough. They could not be fried, so they were boiled and made into chicken salad sandwiches, or chicken and dumplings, or chicken pot pies.

When I was a little boy going to Prices Fork Elementary School, Mrs. Sheppard got on there as a cook. It was a grand day when she came. We started having things like kale greens and pinto beans on Friday with a big hunk of cornbread. Also, about every two weeks she would make an enormous pan of chicken pot pie. It was about half chicken, half peas, and half carrots and all good. Only in Appalachia can cooks be that sure!

Town boys just never got to eat like that.

Here is what you will need:

- Today, you can run over to the Piggly Wiggly and pick up two big pie shells. Or you will have to make them. Grandmother and Momma always made pie shells.3 pounds boiled chicken meat cut into ½-inch cubes. Save the chicken water to make gravy!A pint jar of canned peas and corn. Both need to be rinsed good.
- About a pint jar of both carrots and peas, or fresh carrots and onions pulled from the garden. Make sure the carrots and onions are washed and cut into ½-inch pieces. (On River Ridge, if it was late in the fall, the carrots were buried in mounds with cabbage. In the fall and winter, the onions were out in the smokehouse or cellar tied in small sacks hanging on the wall by a nail.)
- 1 cup whole fresh milk or cream.
- ½ teaspoon salt and ½ teaspoon black pepper. (Salt and pepper to your own taste. Me, I keep the pepper shaker close at hand.)
- From the small herb garden growing by the back door, pick a few sprigs of parsley and sage. Chop them right fine. Again, use the amount you like.
- 1 cup all-purpose flour
- A big saucepan and a baking dish large enough to hold the pie shell and this mixture. Also, remember it is going to grow as the pie gets to cooking.
- Once in awhile you might want to add three eggs. This will make the pie stick together a little better.

Here is what you do:

1. Heat up the oven to 400^0.

2. Melt the butter in a good-size saucepan and cook the carrots and onions a little.

3. Let the saucepan cool down a good bit and stir in the cup of flour and then add in the cup of cream. Now add in the drained jars of corn and peas. (Eggs, too, if you want to use them.)

4. Dump the chicken cubes into the mixture.

5. Sprinkle in the herbs.

6. Dump everything into the waiting pie shells. Again, remember they are going to expand as they cook, so don't fill them all the way to the top.

7. Put a second pie shell on the top of the mixture. Don't forget to poke a few holes in the top crust to let out some steam.

8. Put the pot pie in the hot 400^0 oven for about 20 to 30 minutes, then reduce the heat to 170^0 for another thirty minutes or until fully cooked.

9. It is a good idea to put the chicken pot pie in the center of the oven. This might help keep the crust from browning too quickly.

10. Once in awhile, people will paint the top pie shell with a well-beaten egg to make the crust brown. If you wish to do this, you should do it at the 30-minute mark when the oven is turned down.

Notes for the cook's eyes only:

- Try a big bowl of fresh-picked wild dandelion greens, strong vinegar, yellow cow butter and lots of hot biscuits, small green onions and red radishes with a small pile of salt on the corner of your plate.
- Mashed potatoes and butter round out the meal nicely.
- Cooked turnips with melted butter are great, too.
- If there are any leftover cold slices of bacon from breakfast, this would be a great addition to the meal.
- If you have a lot of leftover mashed potatoes from earlier in the day or last night, now is a good time to make fried potato-cakes. (Some people may choose to add their left-over mashed potatoes to the pot pie mixture. They are good that way, but you be the judge.)If you are eating this in the spring, a rhubarb pie and strong coffee tempered with fresh cream are a treat.

Baked Chicken

One of the worst jobs out there was wringing a chicken's neck, but when I was told to, I went and did it. Well, first off, Mother had already put a very large pan of water on to boil. When it was about ready to boil she would holler for me. I would go to the chicken lot and pick out the oldest hen in the chicken house.

Most likely she was old enough to not be laying eggs anymore anyway. Often I would grab up one with the fewest feathers; few feathers looked old to me. So, I would grab her up and walk out into the yard and set the big zinc tub on the ground and then get the old hen by the head and give it a quick twist. Often her head would come off and the blood would start spurting out of her neck. When that happened, I put her under the tub so the blood did not get on me, too. When it was quiet under the tub, I reached in, grabbed the chicken and took her home to a pan of boiling hot water.

Mom would immerse the chicken in the boiling water, and we would pick off the feathers. Once all the big feathers were removed, I would carry the chicken outside, set four or five sheets of newspaper on fire and hold the chicken in the flames to burn off all the pinfeathers.

Here is what you need:

1 teaspoon cumin seeds

1 teaspoon coriander seeds

1 teaspoon black pepper (You sure can use more if you like.)

1 Tablespoon salt

2 or 3 Tablespoons butter

1 cleaned old hen

5 cups potatoes cut into quarters

A small amount of lard—possibly 2 Tablespoons

2 teaspoons mustard seeds

Here is what you do:

1. Cut the oven on to 325^0 Fahrenheit. (I typed it out to see if I could spell it.)

2. Grind all the cumin seeds, coriander seeds, and black pepper together. (You can put them in a small piece of white cloth and carefully hit them with a hammer a time or two if you don't have an old coffee grinder.)

3. Put the chicken in a big bowl and rub the spices all over the chicken.

4. Take you a big cast iron roasting pan out of the closet and place the chicken in it and then in the oven.

5. Cook until it is done. (Every oven is a little different. If you need to, you can use a meat thermometer. At 155^0 the rascal ort to be done.)

6. While the chicken is in the oven, boil your potatoes until they are about cooked. Take them out of the water and let them cool. Then dry them off.
7. In a second cast iron pan, melt your lard and butter. Add in the mustard seed. (You can use ground mustard seed if you are of a mind to. About one tablespoon is enough.)
8. Add in the potatoes and fry until golden brown.
9. Now take the chicken out of the roasting pan and set it up on a small rack to drain a little.
10. Place the hot potatoes on a big plate and set the chicken on top and serve.

Notes for the cooks eyes only:

- If you want, hot rolls would be good, yellow cow butter is a must and sweet tea is great. If it is late spring, fresh green peas would be a good addition.
- If you wish, a dish of gravy would be nice, too.
- Strong Luzianne Coffee is a good thing as well.

Baked Chicken and Cantaloupe Cubes

This is really good and easy to make. Where I ate this the first time is beyond me. But I do like it. Give it a try and tell me what you think.

Here is what you need:

A large cast iron Dutch oven with a lid

6 chicken breasts

2 8-ounce cans cream of mushroom soup

½ cup water

2 cups ripe cantaloupe cut into ¼-inch cubes

Salt and black pepper to taste

A dash of poultry seasoning, thyme and rosemary

1 Tablespoon flour

Here is what you do:

1. Slowly bake the chicken breasts in the Dutch oven at 400^0.
2. Leave the cover on the Dutch oven.
3. Dump the two cans of cream of mushroom soup into a large mixing bowl and add the water and flour. Stir it some. Taste for seasoning — Salt? Pepper? Herbs?
4. When the chicken breasts are done, remove from the oven and drain most of the fluid from the pan.
5. Place the six chicken breasts back in the Dutch oven and pour the cream of mushroom soup mixture over them.

6. Replace the lid and set the Dutch oven back in the oven for 5 to 10 minutes on a low heat.

7. Just before serving, remove from the oven and add the chopped cantaloupe. Let the mixture stand for one minute.

8. Serve hot.

Notes for the cook's eyes only:

- I like to serve this with brown rice. Have the rice come off the stove at the same time as the chicken.

- This is a right bland-looking plate, so I also like to serve it with pickled beets. (Make sure you drain the beets before serving.) Yellow squash with onions will add a little color, too. A plate with a big flower painted on it might help out.

- The flour makes the sauce a little thicker.

The Red Rooster

About 1960 or just maybe it was 1957, I do not remember the exact date, Uncle Nelson came to my house. He was about 2/3 drunk, but he could talk OK and get around real good. He went into Daddy's bedroom. Daddy had had one or two stiff drinks for sure and may have needed a little time out to recharge.

Wooster (that was a nickname given Nelson by Mod Snider) asked Daddy where his shotgun was. Back in those days, Daddy, Uncle Shorty and Uncle Nelson shared guns. Daddy gets up off the bed and goes to the corner closet and pulls out Uncle Nelson's single shot 12-gauge shotgun and gives it to him. "You and me ain't in no shape to go huntin" said Daddy.

"Hell, Elmer, I ain't going huntin; I am going to kill that old rooster that has been bothering me." Uncle Nelson goes walking down the path toward his house.

Mother comes in the house and jumps on Daddy for giving a shotgun to Nelson. "Nelson doesn't need to be hunting the shape he is in," says Mother.

"No, he is just going to shoot an old rooster that is bothering him."

Mother screams, "Damn you, Elmer. He calls Aunt Tootie 'The Rooster,' and they have been hollering at each other all day."

At that instant both Daddy and Mother take out the front door like their feet are on fire. Me being real nosy, I am close behind. At about 8 years old, I don't want to miss one thing on River Ridge.

We do not get to the line fence gate before we hear the boom of the 12-gauge. Within a few seconds the old gun roars back to life. At the same time, we see Aunt Tootie run up to the road and turn toward McCoy. Aunt Tootie, I am guessing, is fifty years old, but she is running like she is fifteen. BOOM, and she rounds the curve by the pond. BOOM, and she is around the curve at Sam Smith's.

Aunt Tootie never slows down one step and she never misses a step! She is flat out running. To be honest, I never could run like that.

Daddy walks over to Nelson, takes the gun from him.

Everything on the hill quieted down real quick-like. Aunt Tootie stayed away for a few days, then she returned to River Ridge and life resumed its natural ways.

At the time, I thought it was funny to see Aunt Tootie run so fast. I could just think about it and start laughing. Seeing her kind of lean going around the curve like she was riding a 350 Honda at Sam Smith's was always a treat. Real soon, it dawned on me just how serious it was, and Mother and Daddy instructed me never to speak of it again. And I haven't, until one day while writing my first book the evening just came back to the forefront of memory of life along the New River. I sometimes tell people that while I was trying to get myself grown up not everything was funny.

Chicken Thighs Made Famous on River Ridge

Here is what you need:

8 to 10 chicken thighs — if you want, you can remove the bones; go on and cut them out. (Me I don't. After they're cooked, I just let my teeth and fingers do the hard work of removing the bones.)

½ cup flour

1 cup bread crumbs—I just use old bread. Or if there are any old cornflakes on the shelf, they work wonders with chicken. (Cover the crumbs/flakes with some black pepper and a little Herbs de Provence seasoning and lightly toast.)

½ to ¾ cup fresh cilantro. In a pinch, I have used dried cilantro from a can. This works well, but you need less. I would suggest only about 2 Tablespoons.

1 Tablespoon garlic salt

1 Tablespoon black pepper

¾ teaspoon dry sage (Fresh is OK, but you will need more, possibly as much as ¼ cup finely chopped.)

3 eggs well beaten

½ cup butter or lard or olive oil or Crisco (Try the butter or lard first.)

10 ounces cold water

6 or 7 ounces good quality Chardonnay. (Go on, take a long drink after you have measured out the wine you need for cooking. I'll not tell a soul!)

Here is what you do:

1. Turn on the oven to 350^0.
2. Wash the thigh meat in cold water and set aside for a minute to dry off.
3. In a large glass bowl mix the flour, bread crumbs, cilantro, garlic, salt, black pepper and sage.
4. Mix the water and wine and stir it up and set aside.
5. Heat up the butter or lard in a large cast iron skillet. I like to use one of the deep ones. The goodness doesn't splash out as much.
6. In a second large bowl, add in the three well-beaten eggs. Dump the thighs into the eggs and stir them around until all the meat is covered with eggs.
7. One thigh at a time, roll them in the dry flour and spice mixture and carefully place them in the hot cast iron skillet.
8. On medium heat, brown both sides of each chicken thigh.
9. After they are brown, place them in a clean cast iron pan and put them in the oven to finish cooking. You can pour the leftover grease from the first pan into a container for later.
10. Pour the wine and water mixture into the original cooking pan and scrape up all the material from the bottom. Now pour the wine, water and deglazing into the pan with the chicken thighs.
11. Put the lid on the deep cast iron pan and bake at 350^0 for 45 minutes to one hour or until done.

12. If there is any Chardonnay left in the bottle, you can drink it up now!

Notes for the cook's eyes only:

- I don't use chicken breasts. They are too dry. If you must use chicken breasts they will need to be cut up into cubes.
- Now I am not trying to get to bossy here, but I think that you should take the leftover oils, butter and lard from both pans and make gravy with it.
- If you are serving this on Sunday, you ort to have mashed potatoes and hot rolls. During the week hot biscuits would do well. Cornbread would do nicely, too.
- A dish of garden-fresh greens would be a welcome addition.
- Have you thought about macaroni and cheese? It sure would be good.
- A jar of canned green beans with chopped onions would be good, too.
- A tall glass of whole milk is almost a must. Coffee or tea if you like.

Fried Chicken

Like They Make it on River Ridge

Spring, summer, fall or winter, fried chicken was always a dietary staple on River Ridge. I think that a whole lot of people up and down the Ridge ate fried chicken. Secret family recipes for fried chicken were passed from mother to daughter. Often not one word of the recipe was ever written down. The secrets were better guarded than Colonel Sanders' 17 secret herbs and spices.

But there was one common thread to every one of these Sunday fried chicken dinners. It did not matter if the Methodist minister was coming or not, someone had to take that walk to the chicken house and come back with young rooster or two!

Here is a second thought about fried chicken. It could be eaten in one meal. No leftovers meant there was nothing to put up or put in the refrigerator. I think this was a holdover practice from the Depression when most of the people on River Ridge either did not have a refrigerator or still had just a small icebox. Just food for thought.

Here is what you need:

2 young roosters cut into pieces

1 pound yellow cow butter

2 cups regular flour in a large green glass bowl

1 teaspoon salt

1 teaspoon black pepper

1 teaspoon poultry seasoning

Other herbs, too. Mamaw always had lots of herbs in small cloth bags she had dried during the summer. If there are other herbs you like, use them.

2 eggs

One quart buttermilk

2 or 3 Tablespoons lard

6 or 8 pieces popcorn

A deep cast iron Dutch oven

A good strong brown lunch bag

Here is what you do:

1. Put the Dutch oven on the wood stove to get warm. Put the butter and lard in the Dutch oven.

2. Dump the flour into another one of those large green bowls and mix it all up.

3. Set the chicken out on the counter to warm up.

4. Add the salt, pepper, poultry seasoning and your other herbs to the flour bowl.

5. Pour the buttermilk into a small bowl then crack the eggs into it and stir them up real good.

6. Put the popcorn in the butter and lard. When it starts to pop, the Dutch oven has reached its best cooking temperature. YES, you can eat the popcorn.
7. Dump the flour and spices into the paper bag
8. Dip a chicken piece in the buttermilk and eggs and shake off the extra.
9. Put the chicken piece in the paper bag and shake the hell out of it.
10. Put the piece of flour-covered chicken in the frying pan.
11. Fill the pan with chicken.
12. Cook the chicken until it is golden brown.
13. Before you turn the chicken over, you can sprinkle some more flour on the uncooked side
14. Again cook until golden brown.
15. Cook for about 10 or 15 minutes on each side or until done.

Notes for the cook's eyes only:

- The paper bag ain't going to last long, so be quick. Today, I use a one-gallon zip lock plastic bag.
- Me, I put both the flour and buttermilk egg wash in the refrigerator and use both when I make chicken gravy. I only make white milk gravy with fried chicken! (Now, you be the judge of the quality of the flour and the buttermilk/eggs. If you don't want to use the flour or milk after having raw chicken in them, it is ok with me, but you are going to cook both in just a few minutes.)

- You need mashed potatoes, cooked turnips, if possible turnip greens, and hot yeast rolls for a meal like this one.
- Stay with River Ridge tradition and have a big dish of mashed potatoes covered with black pepper.
- A full jar of canned green beans, too.

Spring Chicks

Every spring Grandmother and Uncle Shorty set a bunch of eggs. Once in a while they ordered possibly 100 baby chicks from Sears and Roebuck. The chicks came to the U.S. Post Office at Whitethorn. Mrs. Guynn would call Grandmother, and we would all load up in Uncle Shorty's pick-up truck and drive to the boat landing. The post office was on the riverbank in the community of Whitethorn.

Whatever way they came to the chicken house, the little chicks slept under a big light bulb to stay warm. As soon as they got to eating good, we started pulling grass and clover for them. In just a few weeks, they had doubled in size; some were as big as a tennis ball. They were now on their own to venture out and scratch in the ground for grit, bugs and worms. They came and went at will in the small chicken lot. If you turned them out in the big lot, the "chicken hawks" would pick them up right off the ground. You see a chicken hawk, and everyone on the hill runs for their shotgun. Every baby chick the hawk got was one less future egg-layer or meal of fried chicken.

By summer, you could tell which of the brood were young pullets and which were young roosters. The pullets would be kept for egg-layers, and the roosters found their way to the Sunday frying pan. Homemade fried chicken is as good as about anything you can eat!

On Saturday evening I liked to be gone from Grandmother's. That is when she killed and butchered the young roosters. She would just walk into the chicken lot and reach down and grab the biggest young rooster and wring his head off and pitch him under a zinc tub to flop and bleed out. Then she grabbed the next biggest one.

Chicken and Dumplings

Thinking about roosters makes me think about chicken and dumplings. Chicken and dumplings is a dish that isn't eaten that much these days. People just don't raise chickens in the backyard any more. There was a time when about every house in the country had a chicken house and small chicken lot. Chickens are good about eating up table scraps, June bugs and all the insects that come near to them. Some people like the sound of a rooster crowing in the morning; some do not. If you were one of those people who did not like to hear a rooster crowing at sunrise, about the only solution was to make chicken and dumplings. That would stop the crowing once and for all! A rooster might be tough, but he will cook up just fine.

Here is what you need:

1 real fat old rooster or old hen

4 or 5 bay leaves

Salt and black pepper to your own taste. Me, I go light on the salt and heavy on the black pepper.

½ teaspoon poultry seasoning

½ teaspoon garlic powder

6 to 8 Tablespoons yellow cow butter

½ cup oil

One large cast iron Dutch oven

A big mixing bowl

3 eggs

¾ cup flour

3 or 4 cups regular flour

Here is what you do:

1. Pick, clean and singe the feathers off the rooster.
2. Save back the heart, liver and gizzard.
3. Put the freshly cleaned rooster in the Dutch oven. Chop the liver, gizzard and heart and add them to the Dutch oven.
4. Cover the rooster with at least 2 inches of water.
5. Sprinkle the herbs over the rooster.
6. Put the butter in the water, too. It is my way of thinking that you cannot put too much butter. I like there to be a yellow tinge to the water.
7. Boil the rooster for about one hour on low heat. Keep an eye on the water level. You don't want the Dutch oven to boil low. Cook until he is good and done.
8. When the rooster is cooked to the point the meat is almost falling off the bone, remove it from the Dutch oven and set it on a plate to cool.
9. SAVE THE STOCK IN THE DUTCH OVEN!

10. In the large bowl, mix in the salt, pepper, oil, water. Slowly add in the flour and turn it over and over with a wooden spoon until it is dough.

11. Pick the meat from the bones of the rooster and put it back in the Dutch oven. If the stock needs salt, pepper, garlic, poultry seasoning or any other herb, go on and add it now.

12. Bring the Dutch oven back to a boil.

13. Pinch off pieces of the dough about the size of a hickory nut (or about one inch across). Very carefully drop the dumpling dough into the boiling Dutch oven. Be real careful and don't let the liquid splash on you. Stir the stock once or twice and drop a second dumpling and stir. Repeat this step until the dough is gone or there is no more room for dough.

14. On a low boil, cook 15 to 20 minutes or until the dumplings are cooked.

Notes for the cook's eyes only:

- When dropping the dough, get your fingers close to the boiling water so it doesn't splash on you.
- The size of the dumpling is up to you.
- If you get good at dumpling making, the cooked dumpling will be almost as dry in the center as a biscuit.
- DO NOT remove any of the yellow fat from the rooster. This yellow fat helps to color the dumplings. Dumplings ort to be yellow.
- I like to eat my dumplings with fresh October beans, pickled beets, tangy coleslaw, cornbread and sweet milk.

I just cannot imagine a world where there is no chicken and dumplings. I can't. Today, I think there is a resurgence of the old "country dishes" made more modern. In an art class—well I think that was where I heard it—there was a statement that goes something like: "About everything related to design has been designed. Now we are starting to see newer versions of the same things." Take that for what it is worth. But to that end, here is a new recipe for chicken and dumplings. I call it "Chicken and Dumplings 2.0." Please note there are two stages to cooking the chicken and dumplings: making the dumplings and making the stock to cook the dumplings. Me, I like to make up the stock first and then the dumplings.

Here is what you need for the stock:

6 slices thick-cut bacon cut into small pieces

¼ cup flour

2 pounds fat chicken thighs, cut into ½-inch cubes.

Salt and pepper to taste

2 pounds whole small mushrooms

1 big onion chopped

8 garlic cloves mashed and chopped

¼ cup good white wine, an oaky Chardonnay will do

6 or 8 springs fresh thyme, 3 or 4 sprigs rosemary (strip off the leaves from the stems)

10 cups chicken stock (fresh-made or canned). If fresh run, it through a small food processor/chopper and strain the liquid through a colander.

A very large cast iron Dutch Oven

Here is what you do for the stock:

1. Set the big Dutch oven on the stove eye on medium heat.
2. Cook the chopped bacon until crispy and set it out on a paper-towel-lined plate.
3. Salt and pepper the chicken cubes in a small bowl. Roll them around until each chicken cube is covered with flour
4. Now brown the chicken cubes in the same pan used for the bacon. Cook until golden brown. When done, set them out of the Dutch oven.
5. Dump the mushrooms in the same Dutch oven and cook until you think they are done. I cook them until they are a little brown. Add more salt and pepper if needed.
6. Add the onion to the Dutch oven and cook until it is clear.
7. Add the garlic, wine, chicken stock, bacon, thyme, rosemary, and simmer. If the Dutch oven comes to a boil, lower the heat. You may want to stir a few times. Run the spatula across the bottom of the pan to get all of the good stuff loose.
8. Let the Dutch oven cook for 15 minutes while you make up the dumplings.

Here is what you need for the dumplings:

¾ teaspoon salt

1 cup all-purpose flour (If you use regular flour, add in 2 teaspoons of baking powder.)

¼ teaspoon black pepper

2 large eggs

¼ cup milk

Here is what you do:

1. Dump the flour into a large mixing bowl.
2. With a case knife and fork, cut the mixture until it is a dough ball. You can use your hands if you wish.
3. Squeeze off one-inch balls and drop them into the hot stock. Cook for fifteen minutes
4. Very carefully stir them once in awhile. You do not want the dumplings to stick together. The outside of the dumplings will cook quickly, but not the middle.

Notes for the cook's eyes only:

- This recipe is very easy, and there are lots of ways to vary it.
- Once in awhile, I will boil the chicken off the bone and use that meat for chicken and dumplings.
- Just to make the chicken and dumplings look fancier, I will fry chicken and make rice. I put a serving of rice on the plate along with a piece of chicken and serve the dumplings alongside.

Miss Lilly's Curried Chicken Salad

Now, I must be honest with you here. Me and Miss Lillian have not made curried chicken salad together. I have only watched her and her father eat curried chicken salad. But yes, I have made a lot of curried chicken salad since and I've seen her and her daddy on the couch just eating away, with Lilly smiling with each chew. I now make Lilly's Curried Chicken Salad so I can think back to the smile on her face, the peaceful noise of her chewing and the comfort she exhibited there on the couch with her father.

Miss Lillian is a carnivore in every sense of the word. She likes chicken!

Here is what you need:

3 grilled chicken breasts—use any type of marinade or seasoning you like. For my marinade, I use Italian salad dressing, plus a little salt and pepper to taste.

3 stalks celery

1 cup white grapes

1 cup sunflower seeds

½ cup raisins

1 cup mayonnaise (You just might need more, so leave the jar out.)

1 Tablespoon curry powder

½ teaspoon powdered garlic

½ teaspoon cayenne pepper (More if you like—I like more. but Miss Lilly doesn't.)

½ teaspoon salt (more of you like)

1 teaspoon black pepper (more if you like)

1 head iceberg lettuce

1 medium onion (I like red onion the best.)

Here is what you do:

1. Grill the chicken breasts and put them in the refrigerator. When the chicken is cold, pull the meat off the bone.
2. Chop the meat into ½-inch cubes and put it in one of those big green glass bowls.
3. Cut the grapes in half and put them into the green bowl, then add the raisins, sunflower seeds.
4. Chop the celery into small pieces (1/4 inch). You don't want it to be too big and get caught in your teeth. Add the chopped celery to the green bowl, too.
5. With a rubber spatula, stir the meat and vegetable mixture.
6. Evenly sprinkle the cayenne pepper, curry powder, black pepper, garlic and salt over the mixture.
7. Very carefully mix with spatula.
8. Add the mayonnaise and mix.

9. TASTE, and adjust spices and mayonnaise to get it the way you like it.

10. Cover the green glass bowl with plastic wrap and put it in the refrigerator for a few hours.

11. Chop the iceberg lettuce into one-inch cubes or squares. I save this for last. Some people may not want a lot; some may want more.

12. Finely chop the onion and set aside.

Notes for the cook's eyes only:

- I suggest you refrigerate an hour or two before serving. Somehow this cool period lets the spices come together. Just before serving, you can either stir in the chopped iceberg lettuce or set the lettuce beside Lilly's Chicken Salad so your guests get what they want. Both ways work well.

- Same with the onion: some like it, some don't. On the spices, I try to err on the side of my guests' taste, not mine. But, me, now I like a lot of mayonnaise and lots of curry powder, and I stir in the lettuce and onion.

MAYBE IT'S FISHY, BUT FOR SURE

IT'S GOOD

Trot Lines Gone Wrong

As a little boy and young man growing up on River Ridge right on the bluffs above New River, I learned all things river. Setting trot lines was one of the main things we did for fun and fish. We were always in search of the elusive "catfish." Catfish is best fried or baked or fixed any way you can think of. Yes, catfish are that good. The hard part is catching them ugly rascals.

One of the best ways to catch catfish using trot lines is to set a line baited with crawfish, the little crustaceans that look just like a shrunk-down lobster and that live in every stream in the area. They are fast and hard to catch. You can turn a rock over in a creek bed, and if any crawfish is under the rock it will take out swimming so fast that you can hardly see it. Catching crawfish by hand is a slow-going process. You get two or three true Appalachian Americans together on a creek bank, and you can guarantee a much-improved method to crawfish catching will be devised.

Chuck Shorter has all the needed tools. He had a creek running through his farm with deep water, small pools and most importantly lots of shallow rock bottom. All are great habitat for crawfish. And he had an old "C" Farmall Tractor.

We learned that if someone drove that "C" up the creek slowly it would muddy up the creek and turn over lots of rocks. Crawfish took to running or swimming in all directions. The water would be so muddy that they did not know which way to go. During this time, other people would pull a seine up the creek collecting all the confused crawfish. All we had to do was lay the seine out on the creek bank and sort out the crawfish we wanted. We only took the biggest one—you know, the old grandpa crawfish. We pitched the little ones back into the creek and tossed the big ones into a big trash can full of cold creek water.

Lastly, we set the trash can on the back of the pickup truck, ran by the house to get a holt of the trot lines and grabbed the water dipper for the boat. About 95 percent of the time this plan went off without one problem. Like in life, though, there is always something that will come up every once in awhile.

One time, we had a big trot line fishing weekend planned. We had a big barrel of crawfish caught up, and the trot lines were in great order. A few cases of Blue Ribbon Beer had been purchased. As we went down the "to do" list, I could not think of one thing we needed. We had it all. We jumped into our trucks and drove as quickly as we could to Chuck's grandfather's farm in Pembroke. There we pulled up to the storage shed and took out a few trot lines and drove straight to the river.

The river was very high and running out of its banks. We set on the river bank and looked at the high water rushing by. "Damn, the water will go down and then we can set the trot lines," we all thought. A few hours later the New River was still running full, fast and high. The boxes of Blue Ribbons were getting low. Our stomachs were near empty. The catfish we had great gastronomic plans for had not materialized, but the hunger pains were real and getting louder.

We looked around at each other and almost without saying a word we set the metal barrel upon a few rocks and built a fire under the crawfish. Now to this date, I have never eaten a crawfish, but in a few minutes I was going to. I want you to listen real careful to how we cooked them. Ready? We built a fire under them. That is all we did.

Today when I tell people about this, they look at me like I am one of the natural wonders of the world. Why this did not kill me, I do not know. Most people would have put the crawfish in clean water to wash the creek water and crawfish waste off. We just left them in a big barrel of creek water. Most people would have put a small quantity of water in a big pot —say a gallon or so—and dumped the crawfish in the hot water. This way the crawfish would be cooked very fast, somewhat like a lobster would be cooked. No, we just waited for the water to heat up and a long time later, a lo-o-o-ng time later, the water got very hot. I do not think that it ever boiled.

Once the water got somewhat warm, we started eating the crawfish. They were great! Possibly the great taste came from my hunger and the growing number of Blue Ribbon Beers I had drunk. Some I ate were just a little above warm, but down they went and there they stayed. The next morning the river was back down to normal, but there weren't any crawfish to set the trot lines. We just went on home.

Some years later when I was living in West Tennessee, I ate crawfish again. These were not caught out of the creek, but bought from a man at the supermarket. They were big and meaty.

Crawfish

Here is what you need:

A big outside cooker

A three-gallon aluminum pan—one about big enough to scald a hog in

10 pounds of frozen crawfish that have just been thawed out and washed a few times

2 gallons of salted boiling water

Lots of butter and salt

Lots of sweet tea

Here is what you do:

1. Have lots of tea already made.
2. Bring two gallons of salted water to a boil.
3. Carefully, put the crawfish in the boiling water, filling it to within one inch of the top.
4. Boil for five minutes and set the big pot off the burner and dump the crawfish through a colander.
5. Set and eat with butter and salt.

Notes for the cook's eyes only:

- There is no comparison of the two ways to cook and eat crawfish.
- If you need crawfish for a special recipe, go on over to Kroger and get the fresh frozen kind.

Salmon Cakes with Fish Roe

Momma made this only in the spring when I was catching a lot of small red eyes and perch. I think that we ate a million salmon and mackerel cakes. I just loved them. In fact, I still do. Well, here is another example of Appalachian philosophy of life: "If you got it, you eat it."

Here is what you need:

6 fresh eggs stirred up

¼ cup fresh cream

¼ teaspoon both salt and pepper (to taste)

¼ cup yellow cow butter

1 cup chopped onions

2 16-ounce cans of salmon (no need to drain)

1 large cast iron skillet (Once the doctor checked my iron and found traces of human blood in it, but there was plenty of iron.)

A big glob of lard

A large mixing bowl

8 or 10 sacks of fish eggs washed and drained

3 or 4 cold biscuits

About 6 kernels of popcorn

Here is what you do:

1. Put the lard in the skillet and set it on the stove to get hot and add the popcorn kernels.
2. Over the bowl, break the cold biscuits into a million pieces.
3. Add the salt, pepper, onions and mix.
4. Add the cream, butter and eggs and again stir.
5. Mix in the salmon.
6. By hand, carefully make small salmon cakes. Very carefully work one of the fish egg sacks into the salmon.
7. When the popcorn pops, the lard is hot. After you take the popcorn out, start putting the salmon cakes in the pan and move them around a little to keep them from sticking. Repeat the process until the pan is full.
8. Cook until the outside is golden brown. When the eggs are done, it is ready to eat.

Notes for the cook's eyes only:

- If you want to, you can use canned mackerel. I have eaten both, and I cannot tell you the difference.
- We often ate the salmon cakes for breakfast, so I liked lots of strong coffee, 3 or 4 fried eggs, hot biscuits with butter, homemade jelly, and a tall glass of sweet milk.
- If I was eating salmon cakes for another meal, I liked lots of ketchup, cold biscuits, fresh greens, and coleslaw, too.

Fried potatoes round out the meal. Again cold sweet milk is good, the kind that has been setting in refrigerator for a day or two and has a thick head of cream on it. Just shake it up a little and pour it in the tall glasses.

Mussels from the River

I have begun to think that there are no more stories about life along New River. I guess the human mind is a very complicated thing. Here is what I am getting around to. There are things tucked back into the recesses of your mind that have been floating around for years with nowhere to go, so they just set there hidden from you and the world.

Last week I was leading a seminar for newly retired people. Almost everyone in the room came because they had an interest in writing short stories about their life. Some wanted to somehow put all of their collection of handwritten stories into a book for their family. Some just liked to hear what I was saying and the group's responses.

One of the people talked to me about the New River itself. One of the things he mentioned were the loss of the native mussels that had lived on the bottom of New River.

I had not thought about a New River mussel in fifty years. But now I just could not stop thinking about them. After the workshop, I took out a sheet of paper and made some notes on the subject. Hell, at my age I can forget about anything and did not want this to slip away for another fifty years.

I have three brothers, two younger and one older. The two younger brothers were raised right there on River Ridge, just above the New River. My older brother was a child from my mother's previous marriage. I never knew Tony as anyone other than Uncle Tony. He was a lot older than me and was raised in Richmond, Virginia.

Well, my brother, Tony, came to River Ridge often, but I was very young. (I almost said "little," but I do not think that I ever was truly little. I was once younger.) I have almost no memories of Uncle Tony other than about some weird toys he would bring.

One of the things I do remember was collecting freshwater mussels from New River. We always started by digging out the spring by the big black willow tree down by the White Rock. Daddy and Tony would set two or three five-gallon buckets with large holes in the spring.

Next everyone would pile into the jon boat, and we would paddle to the rock bar and pick up freshwater mussels and pitch them in the boat. They lived all over the river's bottom. Once Tony and Daddy thought that they had enough mussels to fill the buckets in spring, we paddled back to the White Rock.

There, they placed the mussels in the five-gallon bucket resting in the spring. Mussels are filter feeders, so the logic was to let them set in the clean spring water for a few days. This way they could take in fresh clean spring water and not river water. You want your river mussel all flushed out.

After the mussels had spent a few days in cool spring water, Mother, Daddy and Tony would open the shells and take out the meat. This was chopped up and put into potato soup. It was good! Truth be told, I can bet I never ate more than three or four batches of the freshwater mussels in my whole life.

The main thing we did with freshwater mussels was use them for trot line bait. They were that plentiful. I do not want you to think that I stepped on one every step. But every step I could find one. As a kid I loved to go gigging with Mod Snider, Uncle Shorty, Uncle Nelson, Daddy and others. One of the things I can remember and still see in my mind are muskrats setting on the large rocks eating freshwater mussels.

As Mod Snider poled the boat near the rocks, you could see a few shells in the water. Both Mod and Daddy would say things like, "That rascal has been eating those pistol-grip and wavy-backed mussels." Honestly, for years I thought that they were shooting me another line of the kind of bull they were known for. Still, I know they knew something about those New River mussels. Some of the names of them are: "purple wartyback," "pistol-grip," "pock-book," "spike," "wavy-rayed lampmussel," "green floater," and "giant floater."

It is sad, but today almost all the native mussels are gone. Water pollution got some, the buildup to the sediment on the river's bottom got some, and the introduction of other non-native mussels got some. Sadly, I got some too. I do not think that they are all the way extinct yet, but they are damn near gone.

Today, all I can see are those little black ones. The muskrats like to eat them, but I can bet the old-timer muskrats remember those that were the size of half of a cantaloupe setting there on the river's bottom for the taking. I would love to see them once more before I forget again.

Times do change; even the old spring has vanished.

Here is what you need:

A two-gallon or larger stew pot

10 to 15 white potatoes washed, peeled, and cut into bite-

size pieces (You can put two carrots in with the potatoes to add some color.)

3 large onions chopped

1 Tablespoon salt (Later you can add more salt if needed.)

1 Tablespoon black pepper

1 garlic bulb from the barn gate—wash and chop up 10 garlic cloves

½ gallon cream

1 quart freshwater mussels that have been parboiled and chopped up real small. The meat is tough, so the smaller you can comfortably chop it the better.

½ pound fresh yellow cow butter

Fresh herbs from the pots setting next to the back walk

Here is what you do:

1. Boil the chopped mussels until they are done and set aside.
2. Just cover the potatoes with water and set them on to boil with salt, pepper, garlic and other herbs.
3. Add in the cooked mussels and two to three cups of the mussel water.
4. When the potatoes and onions are about halfway cooked, carefully stir in the butter and cream.
5. Reduce the heat to low and let the potato/freshwater mussels simmer for one hour.
6. Every once in awhile, stir it ever so slowly to keep it from

sticking.

7. You want the stew to be thick. Taste once or twice to make sure the spices are the way you want.

8. If the stew starts to get too thick, you can always add more milk, or cream or mussel water. You be the judge!

Notes for the cook's eyes only:

- Please keep in mind that cream and milk will stick real easy.

- I think it is a good idea to make sure the freshwater mussels are totally cooked, too. Them things have little parts as tough as horse harness leather. A little extra cooking won't hurt none.

- Potato soup is always good with canned greens, cornbread, fresh onions and sweet tea.

- In the spring, pick lots of dandelion greens. The bitter taste can offset some of the richness of the Potato/Freshwater Mussel Stew.

Hog Sucker Cakes

As a "Little Fat Boy" on River Ridge, I saw a lot of two things: giggin' and eatin'. As I have stated more than once, my whole family liked the river. By day the whole family went to the river. There we swam, fished, picnicked and played. Come dark, when the long shadows reached a long way into the water, it became a place for the men only. It was like the shadows pulled men and boys to the riverbank.

Sometimes we were raising trotlines and catching catfish. Sometimes we were building big fires out of dry fodder shocks for cooking. Holy macaroni we ate real good! We cooked fresh fish right out of the river, canned sausage, roasting ears out of the garden. Daddy, Shorty and Nelson fried about anything that would hold still or did not run too fast! About the only thing we did not eat was a hog sucker.

At one time, hog suckers were very plentiful in the New River. They have very white meat, and it is very tasty. The problem is, they have more bones than about any other fish in the world. If you fry one you can count on getting a small transparent bone hung deep down in your throat, so far back that Momma can't see it to pull it out. You were forced to eat a lot of hot biscuits with hot gravy. Most of the time this is a good thing; but in this case, the gravy is supposed to lubricate your throat and the hot biscuit is there to force the bone on down into your stomach.

Sounds bad, but not as bad as having Mamma set on you in an old wooden chair and run her two or three fingers down your throat all the way to your Adams Apple looking for a Hog Sucker bone. Often she would just pull out whatever she found. Sometimes she pulled out things other than fish bones!

Daddy did not like gigging hog suckers, because they were so hard to do something with. Also, a hog sucker is fast! When you put the gigging light on one, he takes off like he is riding a 350 Honda. Often they can go two or three different ways at the same time. But when the moon is just right and the River is quiet and the level of the quart jar of mulberry moonshine is steadily dropping, Daddy and my uncles get to thinking, "A few of the hog sucker pieces would make good trot line bait." So they try to gig some.

If they were lucky and got more hog suckers than were needed for trot line bait, they brought them home for us to eat. For most people on River Ridge, other than frying fish there just wasn't much of a way to use up the tub full of hog suckers. My mother, Ruth Lytton, came from Richmond, Virginia. Down there they had two or three pretty good ways to eat fish, other than frying. Mom would make a fish soup and fresh hog sucker cakes.

How do you get the Hog Sucker meat off-n the bones?

Here is what you do:

1. Skin and clean the hog suckers before you ever leave the river bank.

2. Wash the fish in the goodness of New River and take them home.

3. If you do it like Momma, you boil a two-gallon stew pot of

water, then place cleaned hog suckers in a colander and put them in the hot water.

4. The meat falls off the bone. Put the bones in a bucket and the bone-free meat in a bowl that you quickly put in the refrigerator.

5. This does not get rid of all the bones, but it gets a lot of them. You still have to eat real slow, searching with your teeth and tongue for bones. If you miss one, someone is going down your throat looking for the rascal.

Salmon Cakes without the Salmon

Here is what you need:

The sucker meat needs to be dry and cold.

Yes, a large cast iron skillet is used

2 or 3 big dollops of lard are added to the skillet. You want the skillet hot and ready to cook. Please make sure the skillet is well seasoned so the sucker cakes will not stick.

A large green glass mixing bowl

6 or 7 eggs

4 Tablespoons all-purpose white flour

1 Tablespoon salt

1 Tablespoon black pepper

Garlic powder

Any other herbs you can think of

5 or so cups hog sucker meat

Here is what you do:

1. Put the cast iron skillet on the stove to get hot; add some of the lard.

2. While the lard is getting hot, dump the flour, salt, pepper, garlic powder and herbs in the green bowl. Mix all of the dry ingredients.

3. Add the eggs to the flour mixture and stir until there are no lumps.

4. Add in the hog sucker meat and stir until each piece of meat is covered in flour and egg mixture.

5. When the lard is just right, try to make medium-size balls—like meatballs—out of the mixture.

6. Place the balls in the lard and slide them around a little to keep them from sticking.

7. Mash them down some with a spatula.

Turn them over when the sides start to get brown.

Notes for the cook's eyes only:

- They don't always make good balls. Sometimes you will need to use a large spoon or measuring cup to put the hog sucker in the lard.

- They are going to be crumbly, so be careful trying to turn them over.

- Make sure the cast iron skillet is well seasoned.

SIDE DISHES AND BREADS TO ROUND OUT THE MEAL

(AND THE MOMMAS AND POPPAS)

Cornbread to Go with Dandelion Greens

Here is one of the many recipes for cornbread made in Long Shop Style. Dandelion greens and cornbread were two common foods in the spring of my youth. We ate both using many recipes. Today I very rarely eat dandelions, but there was time when I ate them real often.

Here is what you need:

1 Tablespoon olive oil (Lard or butter will work just fine.)

4 cups fresh dandelions clean, dried and chopped

1 teaspoon dry rosemary (I have used dry rosemary from a can for a long time. I just like the smell and taste. If you have a rosemary plant in the herb garden, chop off a small twig or two!)

½ teaspoon of thyme

½ teaspoon red pepper

2 Tablespoons lemon juice

1 cup regular all-purpose flour

1 cup regular cornmeal

2 teaspoons baking powder

½ teaspoon baking soda

¼ cup sugar

1 teaspoon salt

1 ½ cups milk (Buttermilk is best, if you like it.)

About ½ stick butter melted

2 fresh eggs

1 cup canned corn (Put the corn in a colander and drain real good.)

Here is what you do:

1. Turn on the oven to 400⁰.
2. Add the butter to an 8” or 9” cast iron skillet.
3. Put the skillet into the oven to get hot.
4. In a large bowl, combine all the dry ingredients and mix with a fork.
5. In a second bowl mix the eggs, olive oil, and milk.
6. Dump the liquid into the dry mixture.
7. Stir around one or two times.
8. Add the white corn and the chopped dandelions to the mixture and stir around a few more times—don’t over mix.
9. Take the hot skillet with very hot melted butter from the oven and pour the mixture into the hot butter and put the skillet back in the oven.

10. Bake for about 20 to 25 minutes until the top is golden brown or until you think it is done.

Notes for the cook's eyes only:

- I like to serve Dandelion Cornbread with lots of yellow cow butter.
- Homemade coleslaw with a tart taste about it is delicious.
- Shelled beans with freshly chopped onion are almost a must.
- A cabbage-based chow-chow—now that, too, is a must.
- Sweet milk.
- Later in the day, or just before bed, you can take a tall iced tea glass and fill it with cold cornbread and pour cold buttermilk over the cornbread. Top the mixture with thinly sliced green onions and cover the top with black pepper. You will sleep all night long and possibly way up into the morning!

Spring Mushrooms

Gigging fish was something that got Daddy's blood started stirring; he just loved to go giggin'. But one cannot live by giggin' alone. I have tried; I know.

In the days of late winter when the sun came streaming through the bare limbs of the trees and the warm breezes started to blow, the tree limbs started to make moving shadows on the bare ground. It was like a slow-moving announcement of spring. "If you put your ear to the ground or the side of the large oak you could hear Mother Nature saying, "No, I have not forgotten about spring; I like the spring season, too." Mother Nature would whisper this on the breeze to me.

Daddy could hear this call, too. He took to thinking about hunting wild mushrooms. When I was six or seven years old, the whole family along with other people from River Ridge would start hunting wild mushrooms. We were in search of those wild morels you hear about in the gourmet shops. We found very few, but we felt lucky when we could find them. They were wild and free except for all the work we put into walking the equivalence of two or three miles for each morel. Some of the time we never found one. What made me even more tired was finding only one or two. "A day wasted," I would complain.

"No" said Elmer, "you got to breathe the air, didn't you?"

These days as an adult I do not need the thought of fried morels to get out of the house to breath the spring air. You know, the kind of air that ain't been breathed by anyone before!

I bet that I have never eaten more than a half dozen fried mushroom sandwiches. Mr. Gilbert Hilton, one of our family friends, often found wild mushrooms in the spring and brought a few by the house. Gilbert could just see them where I could not.

I now live in town. People are everywhere you look. We have a very small woodshed on the hill behind the house. Last spring, as I pulled the mower out I looked down to see I was standing in the biggest patch of morels I had ever stumbled across. Yes, right here in town. I thought that if I told anyone about the "town morels" the mushroom poachers would be in the yard like the ginseng poachers I've read about. I collected a few, and left some for seed or for spore. I only took the small ones. I cooked them and made a thick sandwich out of town-grown morels. What will they come up with next?

I can just bet that Old Elmer is out there somewhere telling me, "You ort to be walking the mountain looking for the spring mushrooms and quit wasting your time there in town."

As a full-grown adult, I worked for the Virginia Cooperative Extension. Come spring, I always got too busy to mushroom hunt. Well, I like to tell myself that I was too busy. For sure, I was far too important to be seen walking the mountain carrying a small bag, just hoping to find enough morels to fill it all the way to the top. Somehow I seemed to forget about all that un-breathed air and stayed inside with all that about used-up air.

Every once in awhile, a person came into the Giles County Office with a grocery bag full all the way to the top. "Are you the Extension agent man and can you make sure that I have been picking mericals," the person would ask me? (Please note mericals is what I said. That is one of the local names for morel. Murkls is another local name.)

I would carefully dump the mushrooms out on a big table covered in that day's newspaper, pull an Audubon Society Field Guide from the shelf, show my guest pictures of the morels in the field guide and let him or her read about the mushroom.

I started my short inquiry as we worked, looked and read. "Where did you find them?" No answer came back. "Been mushroom-hunting very long?" Only short mumbled answer. "Well, they all look like morels to me."

As I put them back in the paper bags, the inevitable question was, "So, I can eat them?"

Later I learned that there were a few morel hunters that collected the mushrooms for high-dollar restaurants in Richmond, Washington, D.C., and fancy resorts. They needed a second opinion on their stash. I asked for no payment for helping them, and they often left me a few of the broken larger mushrooms. I always thanked them and said nothing to others. But a big mushroom omelet was there for lunch or supper!

Where they collected the mushrooms was a well-guarded secret just like a big patch of matured ginseng is today.

On the subject of a big patch of morels, at one time I was big into planting American Chestnut seedlings. One of our 4-H groups had grown 15 American Chestnut seedlings all winter, and the trees were old enough to plant.

One Saturday morning we met at the Extension Office, loaded up and were off. We started carrying all the digging tools and seedlings up the hill and into the woods. I did a head count, and one of the girls was missing. Sometimes members of the group would step away, out of sight for a few minutes, but after a few more minutes I got a little worried. The whole group went with me to look for her. Within two minutes she screamed, "Watch your step, MORELS!"

She had taken her hooded sweatshirt off and zipped it up to make a carrying sack. It was full of morels. The other adults and I kind of smiled at each other! We took more than 100 nice-sized morels back to the office, where we washed them and set them out to dry off. I made a quick run to the Piggly Wiggly for bread, butter and eggs. This fine morel hunter fried mushrooms and eggs for the group. I think that there is no finer food anywhere! Kids, what can I say? They are about the finest people about, and there is a lot of clean un-breathed air out there. You have just got to go looking for it.

PS: We did plant the trees, too.

Fried Morels

Here is what you need:

A pound of morels (They are light. A pound is a lot of mushrooms.)

Wash in cold water two times and then set on a dish towel to air dry

A cast iron skillet

Lard or Crisco

One egg mixed into a cup of milk

1 cup flour

Salt and pepper to taste

Here is what you do:

1. Have all of your stuff ready. A morel cooks fast.
2. Check over the dry mushrooms and cut the big ones down the middle from the top to bottom.
3. Heat up the lard or Crisco in the cast iron skillet to cooking temperature. This is important. Morels need to sizzle in the lard or Crisco or they will get greasy. If you want, you can put six or eight popcorn kernels in the pan. When they pop the lard or Crisco is up to cooking temperature.
4. Please remember, morels are fragile and will break easily.
5. Roll the morel in the egg and milk and then in the flour.
6. Ever so carefully place the mushroom in the hot pan. Move it around a little. This is done so it will not stick so much.
7. Add salt and pepper to taste.
8. Turn them over when they are brown, making sure you only turn them one time.
9. Serve them hot.

Notes for the cook's eyes only:

- Some of the morels are going to break. You can just fry them and serve them like the whole mushrooms. Sometimes if I have enough, I put the broken ones in spaghetti sauce or hamburgers. They are good with about anything.
- If you want something to make an omelet come to life, add the broken mushrooms to the omelet
- Another thing, they do not need a lot of extra spices. They

are just fine with salt and pepper. But you be the judge of that.

Macaroni Made with Blue Cheese

Aunt Tootie was a pie artist; she was. Her skills did not stop there; she made mouthwatering macaroni and cheese too. Now, Aunt Letty was the unquestioned and undisputed World Master of Macaroni and Cheese! In the grand scheme of things, there have only been two true macaroni and cheese makers—Aunt Letty and Aunt Tootie were about as good as anyone on this earth. I do think the secret to their success was the amount of cheese. Both dishes were so thick with cheese that once in while you had to go looking for the macaroni. I also think butter had a lot to do with it. They used yellow cheese both hard and soft.

The first time I ever ate blue cheese was about 1964. I was up on the ridge above Keister's Branch. It was a very cool night, and the stars were so close that that you had to almost bend over to keep from knocking them out of the sky with your head.

I was with Grat Olinger, Fred Guynn and possibly Mr. Botts. The hounds were loud, running free and clear. This group of old men had a piece of plastic stretched across a wooden block. There they had spread that evening's buffet. There was apples, pears, peanuts, and longhorn cheese, along with hunks of fresh rolled bologna. As I ate my way across the stump I ran into my first piece of blue cheese. I loved it from the first bite. It was salty, some creamy, some bitter and all good.

Once in awhile I would get a piece of blue cheese from the Mick or Mack delicatessen. But I never ate much of the stuff until I moved to Rhode Island. There I found many different kinds of blue cheese. Also, the man at the cheese shop gave me a piece of paper with this recipe for Blue Cheese and Macaroni.

Here is what you will need:

½ stick butter

½ cup all-purpose flour

2 ½ cups milk

1 cup thick cream

3 cups white cheese cut into small ¼ inch cubes

2 cups blue cheese crumbled up

1 Tablespoon fresh chopped rosemary and 1 Tablespoon chopped chives

Each time you cut something, move something over or just touch something eat a small piece of blue cheese. It is good for you.

Here is what you do:

1. Turn on the oven to 350^0.
2. Cook the macaroni until done and drain it.
3. Grease a glass cookware dish with the butter.
4. Put the ½ stick of butter in a saucepan and melt it over low heat.
5. Slowly stir in the flour and keep on stirring.
6. Now stir in the whole milk and cream and keep on stirring.

7. Here is where it gets a little touchy. Add in the white cheese and blue cheese. If it needs salt or pepper, now is the time to add it in, too.

8. When the cheese melts, dump in the cooked macaroni and stir it a few times and dump it all into the buttered baking dish.

9. Bake until the dish is bubbling. You can let it bubble for a few minutes.

10. Take the macaroni and cheese out of the oven and cover with the fresh herbs.

Notes for the cook's eyes only:

- I always think about family reunions when I see macaroni and cheese, so you will need stuffed peppers, and green beans with a few shelled beans in the pan.
- Sweet tea is important, too, along with hot rolls and fried chicken.
- Be ready to write this recipe down for about half of your cousins who are going to want it. The other half? I would suggest you give them some room to learn to enjoy!

Potato Cakes Charles' Style

Truly as an Appalachian American male child living on River Ridge, I ate my share of potato cakes. I have eaten the kind made from cold leftover mashed potatoes. I have had the pleasure of eating those made from fresh boilt potatoes that were kind of lumpy. Both are just plain good.

In our little cinderblock house, potato cakes were made to use up leftover potatoes. But some of the time, they were part of my diet when the month's paycheck was about run out before the month was. We always had potatoes in the well house. Uncle Shorty had a way with words and they packed a lot of meaning. "Hell boy, cold potato cakes beat the hell out of a snow ball."

I complained very little and just kept on eating. Complaining would not have made the paychecks stretch more. I met a fellow who was a few years older than me, and we got to talking one afternoon. He told me that his mother kept their family alive one winter with potato cakes, eggs and lard. She always put a few eggs in the potato batter so the egg would be distributed among all his brothers and sisters. They, too, needed the protein. Life on River Ridge was simply good. A lot can be said for a few acres and big garden!

Today, I think that more people could eat potato cakes and be happy like I was there on River Ridge. I still make potato cakes, but I make them a little different than Mother did.

Here is what you need:

A large cast iron skillet

About a cup of lard

A large green glass mixing bowl

10 good-size firm potatoes

1 pound store-bought bacon

2 large red onions (or 3 green onions tops and all)

3 Tablespoons Dijon mustard—the kind with the mustard seeds in it

3 Tablespoons mayonnaise

3 eggs

1 cup self-rising flour

¼ teaspoon salt (to your taste)

½ teaspoon black pepper

½ pound country ham—chopped coarsely

Here is what you do:

1. Wash and peel the potatoes.
2. Grate the potatoes on a coleslaw grater.
3. Put the grated potatoes in a colander for a few minutes to drain. If the potatoes are still too wet when you get ready to start cooking, dump them out on four of five paper towels.
4. Fry the bacon until crisp, then crumble it up and put it in

the green glass bowl.

5. Finely chop one of the onions and add this to the green bowl.
6. Add the eggs, mayonnaise, mustard and flour and mix.
7. Set the cast iron skillet on the stove with a dollop of lard.
8. Now cut the second onion into ½-inch slices. Place the larger slices in the hot lard to start cooking. Once the onion rings are clear or about half-cooked, start putting the potato cakes into the onion rings.
9. Form a potato pancake from the mixture and carefully place it inside the onion ring. Repeat this until the skillet is full. Cook on medium to high heat.
10. CAREFULLY turn the potato cakes over. Cook for about 4 or 5 minutes on each side.
11. Serve two or three potato cakes to each person.
12. I like to put a piece of chopped country ham on top.

Notes for the cook's eyes only:

- The onion ring will help you hold the shape of the potato cake.
- You can use sausage instead of bacon if you like.
- Sometimes, I will fry eggs to put on top of my stack of potato cakes.

Potato Cakes Revisited

When I was a child we had lots of fried potato cakes. Everyone made them. They were good eaten hot or cold. Mom made them for breakfast, lunch or supper. They were a catch-all food item. All of the leftovers were dumped into the potato cake mixture. Grandmother made that old green bowl of hers almost full of mixture. Sometimes they had corn in them; sometimes they had onion and green pepper. On the River Ridge nothing got wasted.

At Thanksgiving Mother must have boiled 10 to 12 pounds of white potatoes, because she would have enough leftover mashed potatoes to make one or two meals of potato cakes. Mother's were right special. She had made the potatoes with lots of yellow cow butter and whole cream. The mashed potatoes were as yellow as gold. They were also fried in lard. I think the lard gave then a light fluffy taste. Lard is just good stuff. Today I use Crisco, corn oil and olive oil. I think they are just as good as ever. Possibly I am eating my potato cakes, but thinking of Grandmother's and Mother's heavenly creations.

When I was in West Tennessee I ate grit cakes. They were made much like potato cakes. One of the differences was a slice of hot pepper cheese. The second you turned the grit cake over a thin slice of pepper jack cheese was set on the hot side of the grit cake. Guess what? Cheese is great with potato cakes as well. Yes, I put yellow cheese as well as pepper jack cheese on every potato cake.

I do not use grated cheese in the mixture. I find that makes the potato cake stick to the cast iron skillet. Then it makes me want to cry when guests say to me, "That is why I don't cook with that kind of pans. My grandmother muddled away with cast iron. Me, I got me a set of those non-stick pans." They tell me that with their mouth full of potato cake, reaching across the table for the last one. Me, I will just keep putting the slice of cheese on the top.

Here is what you need

10 cups of cold day-old mashed potatoes. The exact volume isn't that important

2 eggs

½ teaspoon salt

½ teaspoon black pepper

½ teaspoon red pepper

½ teaspoon rosemary

1 cup of milk

A large cast Iron skillet

A mixing bowl

Crisco

¼-inch slices of sharp cheese (one slice for each potato cake)

Here is what you do:

1. Dump the leftover mashed potatoes into a large green glass mixing bowl.

2. Sprinkle the dried herbs and spices evenly over the top of the mashed potatoes.

3. With your hand, work the seasonings into the potatoes.

4. Add the milk and eggs to the mixture and again work the mashed potatoes. (If the mixture is now a little soft, this is ok.)

5. Let the potato cake mixture set while you put the cast iron skillet on the stove to heat up.

6. Add at least ¼ cup Crisco. You may need to add a little more so the skillet bottom is well covered.

7. Fill the pan with Potato Cake mixture – Again if it is runny don't worry. When the egg cooks, it will stiffen up.

8. This is important! You need to check and adjust the spices. When the Crisco is very hot, put two tablespoons of the mashed potato mixture in the middle of the cast iron skillet. Slide it around a little to insure it doesn't stick. When it is brown on the bottom turn it over. Slide it around in the Crisco some. ONLY then do you mash the potato cake down to a thickness of about 3/8 inch. Cook until the egg part of the mixture is done. When it is done, take it out of the pan and eat it.

Notes for the cook's eyes only:

- When you start planning a meal, think about the potato cakes and make more mashed potatoes than you will be serving during the meal.

- Look over the herb and seasonings list. You can add any volume or add in any other item you like.

- When making fried potato cakes for dinner, I make them in medium-sized onion rings
- It is very important that you move the potato cake as soon as it is resting on the bottom of the cast iron skillet. You do not want them to stick!

The Gravy!

Come Thanksgiving, to a country boy, "The Gravy" just might be more important than the turkey, so read the recipe real careful-like. Remember you're building gravy!! Gravy just doesn't happen; it is built like a house, one stick of butter, one cast iron pan full of flour and meat stuck to the bottom of the pan. Yes, one brick at a time.

Here is what you need:

All of the drippings from the turkey roster pan

1 cup (or less) flour

½ Tablespoon salt

½ Tablespoon black pepper

½ Tablespoon poultry seasoning

1 teaspoon garlic powder

Some rosemary, thyme and sage

A deep cast iron Dutch oven

½ gallon whole milk (If you like, you may use the potato water or a combination of milk and potato water. You are doing the cooking so. . .)

A high-speed, hand-held chopper

Here is what you do:

1. Let the turkey roaster pan cool off. Don't get burned on Thanksgiving; it is a bad sign—reserve that for a day you can take off from work!

2. Dump all the drippings from the turkey roaster into the Dutch oven.

3. Using one of those hand-held choppers, chop and mix up everything in the Dutch oven. What you can't chop, pitch out. Tyler and me, why, we just chop it all.

4. Taste the dripping to see if more salt is needed.

5. Just because: add some salt, ¼ Tablespoon black pepper, ¼ Tablespoon poultry seasoning, ¼ Tablespoon garlic powder. (More seasonings may be added as the gravy building continues.)

6. If you like, you may dust the top of the drippings with the rosemary, thyme and sage. (Your choice here! But, Tyler and me like the herbs.)

7. Stir in ½ cup white flour.

8. Slowly, pour in most of the ½ gallon whole milk. (And remember, if you want, you can use all or some of the water used to boil the potatoes.)

9. Set the Dutch oven on a large stove eye and bring the gravy to a boil. Stir the whole time! Given the chance, milk will stick. Let the gravy cool down.

10. Taste for seasoning—gravy is built around good firm seasonings! Just remember, the only reason for the

Thanksgiving turkey is to supply the stock for the gravy!!!

11. If you like what you see and taste, set the gravy on to simmer for ½ hour.
12. If you don't like what you taste, adjust your seasonings, then set the gravy on a slow simmer for ½ hour.
13. Keep in mind that the gravy's true thickness will not be realized until it cools down.

Notes for the cook's eyes only:

- Every once in awhile the gravy just might turn out to be lumpy, so here are my suggestions. Put the high-speed mixer on blend, and go to work in the Dutch oven to chop up them lumps. But do this only when no one else is looking! Cooks like Tyler and me don't give away our trade secrets that easy.
- Another suggestion: if the lumps are small ones, don't say anything about them. Just let the eaters think the lumps are from the lumpy mashed potatoes.
- After Thanksgiving dinner, I take all of the bones, the remaining drippings in the pan and the turkey skin and boil that mixture with poultry seasoning, pieces of onion, black pepper and salt. This becomes the turkey stock for soup. I freeze the stock in one-quart jars for use all winter long. The stock can be easily thawed out and made into gravy, too.

SWEETNESS AND LIGHT TO FINISH THINGS OFF

Avery's Christmas Cookies

It is Christmas, and for the first time I am watching Christmas cookies being made. Avery is standing on a kitchen chair with her own little chef's hat sliding down on her head. She has some flour on her apron. She and her mother are mixing up Christmas sugar cookies. After awhile she starts to roll out the dough and cut it into reindeer, Santa Clauses, candy canes, Christmas trees and other shapes.

I return a little later, and the cookies have been baked and are setting out to cool. Sitting around the kitchen table, Avery, her grandmother, mother and little sister are decorating cookies. To me, this is one of the best parts of the Christmas season: a room full of laughter and smiles. Each person trying to make the best-decorated cookie there is. Their pride shows. Every once in awhile, Avery gives a backward glance to see where Mother is, and then when her mother isn't looking, she quickly sticks her fingers in the cookie icing. With red and green icing stuck to her chin, she then gets back to decorating cookies.

Me, I spend my time mostly watching them decorating cookies. Oh, yes, every once in awhile, I sneak one of Avery's cookies off the plate. It is good. There is just something about a cookie made by a 5-year-old.

I once was told that Christmas is for kids. I am now pretty sure that isn't so true. I think Christmas is for us old folks, too. Our presents are different is all I can say. Kids like toys, doll babies and electronic gizmos. Me, I just like to see sugar cookies made to look like Rudolf.

In my family, we had very few "Family Christmas Traditions." We opened Christmas packages on Christmas Eve, watched TV all day Christmas Day and ate a very big meal. I don't think the lack of traditions was because we were poor. I truly don't think of my family as poor. We just did not have any carry-over traditions from either Mother's side of the family or Daddy's. So when I see Avery baking Christmas cookies and watch Avery and Brooke decorating them with icing, it is somewhat new to me, and it is fun to be included.

Here is what you need: (This is for only one batch.)

2 ¾ cups all-purpose flour

1 teaspoon baking soda

½ teaspoon salt

½ teaspoon baking powder

¼ teaspoon cinnamon

1 cup softened butter

1 ½ cups white sugar

1 egg

1 ½ teaspoon vanilla extract

2 mixing bowls

A greased cookie sheet

A flour sifter

Here is what you do:

1. Set the flour sifter in the largest mixing bowl you have.
2. Add the flour, salt, cinnamon, baking powder and baking soda to the sifter. (No, not the sugar. It will be mixed with the butter.)
3. It might not be a bad idea to sift the flour a time or two just to get the ingredients distributed through the mixture.
4. Now set the flour aside.
5. In the second bowl, add the butter and sugar. Then stir until you have a creamy mixture.
6. Add the eggs and vanilla to the sugar and butter and mix.
7. Slowly add in the flour and mix well. Mix until you can form dough balls.
8. Cut on the oven to 375^0.
9. Sprinkle flour on the countertop, and dump the mixture onto the counter.
10. Roll out the dough to about 3/8" thickness.
11. Sprinkle flour on your hands and cookie cutters.
12. Fill the baking sheet with cut outs. If you tear some, don't worry. You can add those to the dough that's left and gather it all back into a ball and roll it out a second time. You want to do that with the scraps of dough anyway, to get as many cookies as you can.
13. Bake at 375^0 until brown on the top, somewhere around 8 to 10 minutes.

14. Set the cookies out on the counter to cool.
15. When the cookies get cool, you can eat two or three with strong coffee or milk, whatever you are in the mood for.
16. Start decorating the cookies with red, white and green frosting.
17. Eat some more!

For the cook's eyes only:

- Here is a suggestion: don't work the dough too much. If you do, the cookies just might turn into crackers.
- Do not forget to put a little of the flour on the countertop and keep the flour on your hands. This is the most important part of keeping your hands and the counter free of dough.
- Stay out of the way as much as you can.

A Simple Apple – Fruit Pie

There were two orchards near The House. Grandmother's home was called "The House." The new orchard was right in front, just above the pond. The old orchard was down over the hill behind the barn and stretched all the way to the holler leading to the cliffs. There were apples, peaches, pears and cherries, too.

Now, we ate apples. We almost lived on apples in the fall and winter. We ate your boiled apples, and jar after jar of applesauce was canned. We made a truckload of apple butter, too. About every morning of my early life there was fried pork—ham, bacon or sausage—and fried apples to go with it.

If a few apples wilted down, they were quickly separated from the other apples and made into fried apple pies or regular apple pies. If there were not enough apples other fruits were mixed in to make enough to fill the pie crust. Yes, we ate apples, but one of my favorites were the simple apple fruit pies.

Here is what you need:

Cut the oven on to 400^0.

8 or 10 apples (I like the hard Stamen and York varieties.)

Peel, slice and core the apples.

3 Tablespoons dark brown sugar

1 pint jar canned cherries

1 cup all–purpose flour

1 cup yellow cow butter

A large oven baking pan or glass dish. It is a good idea to grease the dish with a spoonful of lard.

¼ cup oatmeal

Here is what you do:

1. In a saucepan cook the apples on low heat until they start to get soft. Try not to let them stick.
2. Once the apples are puffed up, let them cool down.
3. Pour in the jar of cherries and mix up the filling and pour the mixture into the cold baking dish.
4. Now put the baking dish into the hot 400^0 oven and let the pie cook for about 25 minutes.
5. In a second bowl pour the oatmeal, flour and butter. Cut this with a fork and a knife until it starts to look grainy.
6. Sprinkle the mixture over the top and bake for another 25 minutes or until the crust is brown.

Notes for the cook's eyes only:

- If there ever was a time for vanilla ice cream, this is it!
- This simple pie can be served with any meal I can think of.

Baked Apples

In the early autumn when apples started to fall, we started to eat them. Grandmother had a baked apple recipe that made all other apple pie recipes stand back and look. This one is simple and quick to make. It might take a few minutes to crack the nuts, but that is ok, too. That is what the cool clear days of fall, just before heavy frost, were made for—setting on a stump cracking walnuts.

Here is what you need:

½ cup black walnuts chopped into small pieces

1 cup of any other nut you have or can find (pecans, almonds, hickory. . .) Just chop these nuts into small pieces, too.

8 good solid tart apples, 4 red and 4 yellow ones

½ cup dark brown sugar

¼ teaspoon cinnamon

½ teaspoon salt

3 cups oatmeal

1 cup Karo syrup (any syrup will do. Today, I use maple syrup.)

1 pound yellow cow butter (Please don't tell anyone, but I get my butter from the Kroger Store.)

A large baking dish or pan

A few little pieces of caramel, if you have it. If you don't that is ok; don't make a special trip to the store over it.

Here is what you do:

1. Go on and turn on the oven to 350^0.
2. Chop up all the nuts and dump them into a large mixing bowl.
3. Into the same bowl dump the brown sugar, cinnamon, salt, and oatmeal. Mix all these dry things together.
4. Add in the butter and syrup and mix the best way you can. You do not need to mix it up too much.
5. Grease the bottom of the pan with a little butter.
6. Cut the core out of each apple making a real big hole. DO NOT peel the apples. Also, you just might need to cut a small slice off the bottom to make them stand up straight in the pan.
7. Stand up each apple in the baking pan. It is ok if they touch.
8. Carefully start filling each apple with the filling. Put the little caramel pieces in about the middle of each apple. Press it down with your fingers. Try not to let the filling run down over the sides into the pan. If you have too much filling left over, just core another apple or two.
9. Bake uncovered for 30 minutes.

10. When you take the apples out of the oven you can top them with a few more nuts if you like.

Notes for the cook's eyes only:

- Vanilla ice cream.
- Call me old-fashioned, but I am one of those people who like sharp cheese with apple pie.
- This a great complement to brown beans, hot rolls with lots of yellow butter, freshly made coleslaw, canned beets, fried potatoes with onions and turnip greens.
- If you are eating this for supper, I strongly suggest coffee with cold, thick whipped cream. That is just a suggestion. You can drink about anything you wish, but I like coffee.

Blackberry Cobbler

As a little fat boy growing on River Ridge I ate tons of cobbler pies. We always had a lot of cream and milk. In the early summer the berries were all over the hillsides and fat little boys have to eat something. As most people already know, I am the last of the true blackberry pickers and I know cobbler.

There are many different recipes for blackberry cobbler. I have found this one to be good. All I ever needed was a most willing mother or grandmother! I could do the rest.

Here is what you need:

2 ½ cups fresh whole blackberries

2/3 cup white sugar

1 ½ cup flour

1 Tablespoon baking powder

½ teaspoon salt

1 full cup butter

½ cup cream for whipping

A deep baking dish greased to the top with butter

A mixing bowl

Here is what you do:

1. Turn the oven on the 350^0 to warm up.
2. Make sure the shelves are adjusted so the baking pan will fit. (I did not do this one time and had to move a very hot oven rack. This will make you need to go to church on Wednesday night, and Sunday too.)
3. In the mixing bowl add the flour, baking powder, and salt. Mix! Go on and sift the dry stuff if you like.
4. Now add in the butter and cut the butter into the flour until it forms a real rough-looking dough.
5. Add in the cream and keep on cutting it into the flour until the dough is thoroughly incorporated and looks smooth.
6. Dump the blackberries into the baking dish and pour the sugar over the top. Mix a little bit.
7. Evenly spoon the dough over the berries.
8. Now pour a spoonful or two of butter over the top of the dough.
9. Put the cobbler in the oven for 30 minutes. If it needs a little longer, that is OK. Just cook the cobbler until it is done.
10. Whip the cream a few minutes before you are going to serve the cobbler.

Notes for the cook's eyes only:

- There is nothing special about a cobbler. Add to the recipe and improve as you wish.

- I always whip more cream than I think I will need. Just between me and you, I also keep a can of that Reddi Whip on hand. I have one of those small, hand-held mixer/blenders, so I put whipped cream on everything.
- I just love cobbler with a thick layer of whipped cream accompanied by a cup or more of strong coffee.
- I never turn down cobbler and vanilla ice cream.
- As for other foods to serve with a cobbler, it needs nothing.

Chocolate Gravy
Yes, Chocolate Gravy

Being of true red-blooded Appalachian American origin, my family made gravy out of everything, even chocolate. Now please don't laugh too hard until you've tasted chocolate gravy.

Just take two or three hot yeast rolls out of the baking pan as soon as you can handle them. Pull them in half quickly as you can, put a large hunk of yellow cow butter between the two halves. Do this fast so not so much of the steam is lost. I set them rolls in a soup bowl for the butter to melt and the roll to soak up as much butter as they will. I like to do this a few minutes before the chocolate gravy is finished so everything is hot and packed with goodness at the same time. When the gravy is finished spoon 8 or 10 big spoons of gravy over the rolls. Enjoy!

Back in 1950, I think cooks were more creative than those today. Old timers knew how well pork fat and chocolate paired together. Everyone once in awhile Grandmother just wanted something different and chocolate gravy filled the bill.

Mark my words on this. One of these days you and me are going to be kicked back on the couch watching the TV. The cooking channel for sure. And the TV cook is going to tell you that he or she has just invented something new, different and great. They are going to tell me to go on and find a pencil and some paper because: "You are not going to believe what we will be cooking after this next commercial and you are going to want to take notes. We are going to make chocolate gravy!"

Here is what you need:

15 or 20 Hershey's kisses

¼ cup yellow cow butter

(7 or 8 Tablespoons of clear bacon drippings will work, too. It is best to skim off the clean bacon drippings as the bacon fries.)

½ gallon cream

Some water

1 teaspoon salt

¾ cup white flour (You may need less; I don't know.)

A large cast iron Dutch oven

Here is what you do:

1. Put all the butter and bacon drippings into the Dutch oven and set it on the stove.
2. Melt the butter and mix together drippings.
3. Once the butter is bubbling hot, set the Dutch oven off on the counter.
4. Add in the flour and slowly stir in the whole cream.
5. Once the gravy is slowly bubbling, set the Dutch oven on a cool side of the stove.

6. Slowly drop chocolate until it is melted into the gravy. Keep on stirring!

7. Put the Dutch oven back on the stove and bring the temperature of the mixture up, BUT DO NOT LET IT BOIL

8. You may add in more cream or a little more milk. Let the gravy simmer for a little while.

9. Be careful. Chocolate gravy will stick real easy!

Notes for the cook's eyes only:

- If you like chocolate gravy, please play with this recipe some. You can add in more chocolate or less; it is totally up to you. Again, it is best with cream and not water.
- I like chocolate gravy on Sunday morning poured over hot fresh rolls right out of the oven. Put a big hunk of yellow butter on the roll. As soon as the butter melts down onto the plate, pour chocolate gravy over the top. It is better than about anything you have ever eaten.
- This gravy can be put on toasted white bread, cold or warm biscuits.

P.S. I know a little vegan girl who will only eat the bacon fat. She just does not like the red part. You just wait a while, and you are going to see pork fat come back into style and everyone will be placing a small jar that looks like a flower pot with no hole on it on the stove for leftover bacon drippings for frying eggs, adding flavor to turnip greens or finishing off a pan of cornbread. Until then, I will keep sneaking around and making a bowl of gravy about every other month and pouring it over light bread for breakfast.

Rice Pudding

As a little fat boy on River Ridge, I ate a lot of Rice Pudden. Not until I was older did I ever eat "Rice Pudding." We ate Rice Pudden, and it was good. I think rice was a cheap staple and with seven mouths plus all the visitors, rice was the way to go. Also, Mom and Daddy thought that if they could keep you fat you were OK. Fat hogs were prized, and a beef with heavily marbled meat was the most tender. So why not keep a "fat little boy" there on the hill? Well-rounded meant very happy. I think this just might be true; I was round and very happy.

Another thing about Rice Pudden. I liked setting on the stool by the long table at Mamaw's house and grating up the lemon peel on the coleslaw grater. I can think back and hear: "Watch your finger on that grater. We don't need any meat in the Rice Pudden." After I was finished, she would take her old finger and run it across the grater and get each piece of lemon peel. Then she cut up the lemons and made real sweet lemonade. Holy Macaroni, I had it made.

Here is what you need:

2 cups white rice

4 cups water (or thereabouts)

2 cups whole milk

5 eggs

1 full cup white sugar

2 teaspoons vanilla extract

2 teaspoons grated lemon peel

2 or 3 spoonsful of yellow cow butter for greasing the baking pan

2 cups of fresh cream (Go on and set the cream out to warm up when you get the other ingredients out. Room temperature cream whips up easier.)

One large baking dish

Some cinnamon for sprinkling on the top of the rice pudding

Here is what you do:

1. Cut the oven on to 350^0.
2. In a large saucepan, add the rice and water, bring it to a boil and quickly reduce the heat to low. Cook covered.
3. Cook the rice about 25 minutes or until tender.
4. In a large green glass mixing bowl, mix in eggs, sugar, vanilla extract and lemon peel. Stir until creamy looking.
5. Today, I like to froth the milk until it is fluffy but not made into whipped cream. I have two of those small hand-held mixers/blenders, and this gives me a chance to use one of them.
6. Butter the baking dish and carefully spoon in the "Rice Pudden" and put in the hot oven.

7. In about 15 to 30 minutes, take the "Rice Pudden" from the oven and let it cool for 30 minutes.

8. When the "Rice Pudden" is cool, beat the cream into whipped cream and carefully mix it in.

9. Sprinkle the cinnamon on the top before serving.

Notes for the cook's eyes only:

- There must be a thousand ways to make rice pudding, but this one has always worked for me. People often ask for this simple recipe. Simple is best.

- Whipping the milk just seems to make the rice pudding more fluffy and not so heavy. I eat less when it is fluffy.

- Some folks even make a second bowl of whipped cream and serve that alongside the rice pudding. When I do this, I put ¼ of a drop (NO MORE) of vanilla in the cream before whipping it. Now that will eat right where you hold it!

Bananas

I do wish that I could lay claim to this story, but I cannot. A year or so ago, I was working with a group of adults. One of the older ladies in the group came up to me after the workshop with a story she wanted me to hear. You will never know how often this happens to me today. Well, since the lady was at least twenty years my senior, I sat down to listen and give her my full attention and respect. One of the funny things about all this is that I can remember her story.

But I only think her name was Lucy May Clyburn. If I am wrong, I am sorry. I sure am glad that I sat down! Lucy May asked me to write this story and to tell it to other groups of people. "Put it in a book if you like," she offered. Lucy May Clyburn was not part of the story; she just remembered her uncle telling it.

The story took place in the late 1920s in the community of Merrimack, Virginia. Please remember I wasn't there; I am just answering the request of an old lady I met. Merrimack had been a coal-mining community for the past 100 years and was a thriving rural place. There was a deep mine that employed a lot of people. There was a spur that ran from Merrimack to the Virginian Railroad. The mine owned a coal tipple and a dinky steam engine pulled coal hoppers from the coal mine to the railroad. [A dinky is a very small steam engine or locomotive. It often runs on a narrow-gauge rail system. Its function was to move light loads from one location to another, like pulling coal hoppers to the coal cars.] There was a coal tipple where the dinky pulled coal hoppers over to waiting Virginian Railroad coal cars and emptied the hoppers into them.

Lucy May's uncle's job was driving the dinky. On one trip from the mine to the railroad, he met a group of boys playing on the coal pile. On his way back to the mine, he saw the boys were still playing in the coal dirt. Uncle stopped the dinky and called for the boys. "Boys you are plum filthy, and you ort to find yourself somewhere else to play. A bath with lots of lye soap would not hurt you either. I am going to make you a deal. I am off work for the next few days, and when I come back if I find you clean, I will give each of you a banana."

Three days later Lucy May's uncle's break was over, and he came back to work. True to his word he had a long hank of bananas. A whole crate of bananas had been delivered to the mine commissary. After a trip or two down the narrow-gauge railroad track to the coal cars, he saw the boys.

But, the boys had seen him first. Off the coal pile they came. They stripped down buck necked on the creek bank and jumped into the swimming hole. In warmer weather, coal miners often took a bath in the same spot. The boys scrubbed themselves there with a bar of strong lye soap, and when the dinky came chugging by the almost-clean boys were standing "buck-necked" on the side of the dinky tracks. Uncle stopped the small steam locomotive and true to his word, he gave each boy a ripe banana. The boys sat their necked butts down on the cross ties and peeled out their bananas and enjoyed this most wonderful gift.

Please don't think that this was the first banana the boys had eaten. It most likely wasn't. Back in the 1920s the roads all over the country were poor. Shipping bananas from Florida to Merrimack took a long time, and they most likely would spoil before they reached the mining communities far off the beaten path in Appalachia. So a banana was a true treat. A treat worth taking a bath over!

Today, I take for granted just how close Florida is and how easy it is to get a banana. If I want to, I can jump in the car and be in Florida in one day. Another thing: you and I can go to a grocery store and purchase a poke of bananas any day of the week. Times, roads and foods have surely changed over the last 50 years. When we went to the Piggly Wiggly for groceries I can remember seeing bananas, but Momma and Daddy did not get them every visit. Once in awhile they were purchased for making banana pudding. Bananas were for special occasions.

When I was about 6 or 7 years old Mother or Grandmother would make fried chicken for lunch on Sunday. Often the meal would include banana pudding, and we all thought that this was some exotic food.

Aunt Tootie could cook a lot of good foods. She was a good pie baker. She made a great macaroni and cheese. Aunt Tootie was a track star, too. But she could make a banana pudding that was wonderful. She always covered the top with a real thick layer of whipped egg whites. Then she put the banana pudding into a hot oven for a few minutes, just long enough for the peaks of whipped egg whites to turn a golden brown. Her banana pudding was real thick, too. Today, when I go out to eat and see a banana pudding on the buffet or menu, you can bet that I will be first in line for a serving!

Here is another little short banana story not from me, but from an old grocery shopper I knew.

A long time ago, right after I graduated from high school, I took a job at the Mick or Mack Grocery Store in Blacksburg, Virginia. I worked in the produce department as the chief potato, fruit and vegetable man. That meant I was responsible for the banana display, too. No, I was not allowed to eat that many, but I did keep the display clean and stocked with the best yellow bananas the delivery man brought to the store. I took lots of pride in the banana display!

Now this story was told to me by a customer. I honestly never learned the man's true name. I will name him "Mr. Mack Beebee" for the purpose of this story. You could tell by the way that Mr. Mack Beebee dressed and the way he spoke about life in general that he grew up hard and knew the meaning of a hard day's work. I think that he must have lived the kind of life so often depicted in many of the older Appalachian stories. You know: poor pay, long dirty hours, big family and so on.

Every once in awhile, my most beautiful banana display would start to have a dowdy look about it. The beautiful yellow bananas that I wasn't allowed to eat started to get lots of brown spots, so I would pull the bananas off the shelf and mark the price way down so someone would buy them and take them home and make banana bread out of them.

One day, Mr. Mack Beebee strolled by the old bananas and took a long hard look at them. He said to me, "Boy, you know I'll just take all them." I carefully set the packages of old bananas in his grocery cart. A few weeks passed, and Mr. Mack Beebee came to the produce department door and asked if I had any more old bananas. I did have a few, and he bought them.

The next time he came in the store I went to the beautiful banana display and pulled all of the speckled old bananas off the shelf and was ready to sell them when he passed. When I said, “Hello,” he just walked over to me as I set the bag of old bananas in his grocery cart.

“You know, when I was about 15 years old I had done quit school and was working deep in the mines as a man. But I was still living under Mother and Pap’s roof, so I still lived by their rules. Some of them rules was right tough. I had done quit school to do a man’s job in the Merrimac Coal Mines. Down at the company store I stumbled across a small box of over-ripe bananas and bought them for a dime. My first plan was to carry them home to share with everyone, but the closer I got to home the better them bananas smelt. I set down under a big tree by the road and ate the whole box.

“I must have ate twenty or more bananas. I ate so many that I was kind of sick. Pap came walking by and asked me what was wrong. Without thinking I told him about the bananas. Pap got so mad that I thought he would explode!! He grabbed me up and tied me to the fence there by the big tree and proceeded to beat them bananas out of me. ‘I will teach you to be so damn greedy and selfish!’ he screamed.

“The beating was over as quick as it had started. Pap did more screaming than hitting. To this very day I never eat many bananas; I just don’t have a taste for them. I think that is because I never see a banana that I do not see the anger in my Pap’s eyes. These days, I take all of the old speckled bananas to my grandkids. I ask them to eat the bananas until they run out of their ears, and I just laugh. Sometimes I give them a case knife and a jar of crunchy peanut butter, too. They can eat up a gallon of peanut butter with old speckled bananas if they want. Sometimes I set down on a bench and eat with them. But Pap’s eyes would not let me eat my fill.”

Now, you can believe Old Mr. Mack Beebee’s story if you like, but I believe each and every word.

OK, here is a short banana story on me. Jay Lee Wall and I are maybe the only two people that remember this story about bananas. I was once a high school football player. In the summer of my junior year of high school, I went out for the football team. I was second string some days and third string other days and other days they did not want to give me a uniform. Yes, you are right, I did not play a lot my junior year.

One afternoon, we were off for a long ride to an away football game. I had previously been instructed to pack a lunch or supper. I did pack this bag lunch, but come suppertime on the bus, my poke was already empty. So when the bus stopped I thought that I should pick up something else to eat. I got off the bus and started to look around, and there was a big banana display. I picked up a hank of bananas. I got enough for supper and a snack on the bus ride home. The hank was also big enough for a snack on the walk back to River Ridge. There was even enough for a before-breakfast snack the next day. When I got to the bus, I stuffed this mountain of bananas in my poke.

When it was announced that we should eat a little from our picnic lunches, some slowly unwrapped a sandwich or started to chomp on an apple. Before the meal was finished, I had eaten my whole poke of bananas. I was a little green around the gills, too. Jay Lee said, “How did you eat all of them bananas?” I could walk, but I had a hard time bending over doing the other exercises. Jay Lee still laughs at my banana episode to this day.

No, they did not have to beat them out of me, but I sure was glad when I made a quick walk to the Johnnie house the next day. I still like bananas, but rarely do I eat a whole sack full. I also wonder what would have happened if I had been called upon to go into the game. You just never know. On the first tackle, I might not have needed to take that long walk in the cool morning air. Now wouldn't that make a story in a memory?

For me, banana pudding is an expression of the good life. I bet you ask 12 people about their memories of banana pudding, and the answer will almost always come back an expression of a great memory of family or of time and place they just do not want to forget. All of these thoughts are true for me! Here is a recipe for a banana pudding that I have made and still make for special events—like the picnic at the County Fair or a family reunion. Also, about every family makes it differently, and all ways are right.

Banana Pudding: Charles' Style

Here is what you need:

A real big glass bowl or Corning dish to make the banana pudding in—something that will hold a gallon or more. Yes, you will need something big. We are talking about Lyttons here, not people from town.

A smaller green glass bowl for mixing in

10 or 12 speckled yellow bananas or more

2 large boxes vanilla wafers

2 8-ounce packages cream cheese

1 16-ounce tub sour cream

2 cans Eagle Brand Sweetened Condensed Milk

3 large boxes vanilla pudding

2 small plastic tubs Cool Whip

2 teaspoons vanilla extract

Maybe 2 cups of coconut

Here is what you do

1. Set both boxes of cream cheese out on the counter to warm up.
2. Make up all three boxes of vanilla pudding following the directions on the side of the box. Put the pudding in the refrigerator to stay cold.
3. Get the BIG bowl out, but don't do anything else until the cream cheese is up to room temperature. It needs to soften enough to mix.
4. In the smaller green glass bowl, put the cream cheese, vanilla extract and the two cans of milk. Mix until the cream cheese is mixed up with the milk. Now add in the vanilla pudding. Mix in the sour cream. Fold in the Cool Whip.
5. In the large bowl, put a layer of vanilla wafers, a layer of thickly sliced bananas, a layer of the vanilla pudding mixture and lightly sprinkle with coconut. Do this over and over again until the pan is full.
6. Put the mixture in the refrigerator for two or three hours.

Note for the cook's eyes only:

- I always mix up all the leftover bananas, vanilla wafers and vanilla pudding mixture in the small bowl and set right down and eat it. That just might keep me out of the refrigerator for a little while.

- You can seerve banana pudding with any food you can think of.
- You can leave out the coconut if you like.
- I think the two hours in the refrigerator is important.

Epilogue

For about as long as I can remember I have been cooking and watching my mother, aunts, uncles and grandmother cook. Why, the whole family cooked and they were good at it, too. If you don't believe me set at my brother Melvin's or my cousin Kevan's table! Just like the little boy from River Ridge that I was, I watched and remembered. I took all of these experiences to heart.

Cooking is different in each home and with every person. To make my point, my mother made the best potato onion soup out there. It was about half potato, half onion, half cream and at least half butter. I would even eat a bowl of her potato soup cold. I told this to a lady one time and she answered me, "I like vichyssoise, too." It took me a long time just to find out how to spell vichyssoise. I learned that I can make potato soup fancy by changing its name, not the ingredients. I have eaten lots of hot potato soup and some cold vichyssoise out of the same bowl.

Very early in my adult life, I lived in a small cinderblock cabin on the bank of the New River and had only one old, used cast iron frying pan. I had a big garden, fish from the river and deer from the pastures leading over to the apple trees. I truly did not go to the store except for salt and pepper and other things that I could not grow. I have to admit part of this lifestyle was by choice, but there also were financial constraints. I was working on a local farm and had only enough money for house payments, the electric bill, beer and of course some shine. So I had to be resourceful.

Sadly, I still gained weight. Just maybe it was because I ate a lot of fried potatoes and drank gallons of whole milk from the farm. Maybe my weight gain was because I ate too much of about everything. I enjoyed cooking everything that I ate. Meal menus were full of dishes like fried green apple pies, fried green tomatoes, chicken-fried deer steak and baked potatoes. Or maybe fish rolled in flour and cornmeal and fried in butter or lard, lots of greens, boiled potatoes, cornbread and tomatoes fixed about every way I could think of. I also found that I liked fish soup with chopped onions, green beans cooked with lard, a slice of cured ham. Fresh potatoes with lots of butter was damn good.

Today, I stop and think that I am like my father and Uncles Shorty and Nelson—they all carried one of those small containers (one about the size of your thumb) of Morton's Salt with them about everywhere they went. They could graze all afternoon in the garden eating green onions, fresh green peppers, dusty cucumbers and red ripe tomatoes with just the lightest touch of salt. Me? I can, too.

In these modern times, I still cook at home! I still am fat, too. One of these days I am going to go on a diet. But to date I have not found a diet plan that is high in salt, butter, lard and cream and low on the bad stuff like lettuce. I do question what a body is to do. I guess just eat and enjoy cooking.

I'm hoping that even if you are too busy to read this book cover to cover, you have taken a few minutes to set down and look through it a second time and more importantly cook up something! You will find me right there on each and every page along with a lot of my family. Cook, read and enjoy!

45408678R00156

Made in the USA
Middletown, DE
03 July 2017